ESSENTIAL
RUSSIAN
GRAMMAR

ESSENTIAL
RUSSIAN
GRAMMAR

BRIAN KEMPLE

DOVER PUBLICATIONS, INC.
NEW YORK

Essential Russian Grammar is a new work, first published by Dover Publications, Inc., in 1993.

Manufactured in the United States of America
Dover Publications, Inc., 31 East 2nd Street, Mineola, N.Y. 11501

Library of Congress Cataloging-in-Publication Data

Kemple, Brian.
    Essential Russian grammar / Brian Kemple.
        p.   cm.
    Includes index.
    ISBN 0-486-27375-X (pbk.)
    1. Russian language—Grammar. 2. Russian language—Self-instruction. I. Title.
PG2112.K45   1993
491.782'421—dc20   92-20999
                                                 CIP

CONTENTS

INTRODUCTION

Essential Russian Grammar assumes that you have a limited amount of time at your disposal to study Russian and that your objective is simple everyday communication, both spoken and written. This book, therefore, does not attempt to offer a complete outline of all aspects of Russian grammar, even in a highly condensed version. It does, however, offer a series of aids to help you use more effectively phrases and words that you have already learned. The book will introduce you to the most common structures and forms of Russian and a selected number of the most useful rules.

HOW TO STUDY *ESSENTIAL RUSSIAN GRAMMAR*

If you have already studied Russian in a conventional manner, this book will serve as a review, and you can use it by glancing through all of it quickly and then selecting those areas on which you wish to concentrate.

If, however, this is your first acquaintance with Russian grammar, the following suggestions may be of help:

1. Before beginning to work your way through this book, master several hundred useful phrases and expressions such as you will find in any good phrase book or in the *Listen & Learn Russian* course. The material in this book will be much more easily understood after you have achieved some simple working knowledge of the language. This book's purpose is to enable you to gain greater fluency once you have learned phrases and expressions, not to teach you to construct sentences from rules and vocabulary.

2. Read through *Essential Russian Grammar* at least once in its entirety. Do not be concerned if some of the material is not immediately clear; what appears to be discouragingly complex on first reading will become much simpler as you progress in your study. The first reading is necessary to acquaint you with the terms and concepts used from the beginning. Learning these will help you improve your comprehension of Russian and use more freely the expressions and words you already know. As you use Russian and hear it spoken, many of its grammatical patterns will become familiar to you. *Essential Russian Grammar* helps you discover these patterns, and it will be helpful to you as you develop your vocabulary and improve your comprehension.

3. Go back to this book periodically. Sections that at first seem difficult or of doubtful benefit may prove extremely helpful as you progress further.

4. For the most part, *Essential Russian Grammar* follows a logical order, taking up the major divisions of grammar in sequence. You will do best to follow this order. However, you may be one of those who learn best when they study to answer an immediate question or need (e.g., how to form the comparative of adjectives; how to express the future tense; etc.). If you are such a student, turn to the section that interests you at the moment, but read through the entire section and not just an isolated part. Individual remarks, taken out of context, are easily misunderstood and may seriously mislead you.

5. Examples are given for every rule. It will be helpful if you memorize them. If you learn all of the examples in *Essential Russian Grammar,* you will have encountered the basic difficulties of Russian and studied models for their solution.

6. You cannot study Russian or any other language systematically without an understanding of grammar, and the use and understanding of grammatical terms is as essential as a knowledge of certain mechanical terms when you learn to drive a car. If your knowledge of grammatical terms is a little hazy, read the Glossary of Grammatical Terms (page 94) and refer to it whenever necessary.

In Russian, as in any language, there are potentially many ways to express a single idea. Some involve simple constructions, others more difficult ones. Some of the more difficult constructions may well be more sophisticated ways of conveying the thought and ones that you will ultimately wish to master, but during your first experiments in communication in Russian, you can achieve your aim by using a simple construction. Be satisfied at first with the simplest.

You should not, however, be afraid of making mistakes. The purpose of this book is not to teach you to speak like a native but to allow you to communicate and be understood. If you pay attention to what you're doing, you will find that eventually you make fewer and fewer errors. Sooner or later you'll be able to review *Essential Russian Grammar* or a more detailed book at a time that is appropriate for polishing your speech.

As you begin to speak Russian, you will be your own best judge of those areas where you need most help. If there is no one with you, you can practice by speaking mentally to yourself. In the course of the day see how many simple thoughts that you have expressed in English you are able to turn into Russian. This kind of experimental self-testing will give direction to your study of Russian. Remember that your purpose in studying this course is not to pass an examination or receive a certificate, but to communicate with others on a simple but useful level. *Essential Russian Grammar* should not be thought of as the equivalent of a formal course of study at a university. Although it could serve as a useful supplement to such a course, its primary aim is to help adults study on their own. Of course, no self-study or academic course, or even series of courses, will ever be ideally suited to all students. You must rely on and be guided by your own rate of learning and your own requirements and interests.

SUGGESTIONS FOR VOCABULARY BUILDING

1. Study words and word lists that answer real and immediate personal needs. If you are planning to travel in the near future, your motivation and orientation are clear-cut, and *Listen & Learn Russian* or another good travel phrase book will provide you with the material you need. Select material according to your personal interests and requirements. Even if you do not plan to travel to Russia in the near future, you will probably learn more quickly by imagining yourself in a travel situation.

2. Memorize by association. Phrase books usually give associated word lists. If you use a dictionary, don't memorize words at random but words that are related in some fashion.

3. Study the specialized vocabulary of your profession, business or hobby. For example, if you are interested in mathematics, learn the wide vocabulary in that discipline. You will quickly learn words in your own specialty and a surprising amount will be applicable or transferable to other areas. Although specialized vocabularies may not always be readily available, an active interest and a good dictionary will help you get started.

LIST OF ABBREVIATIONS

The following abbreviations are used in *Essential Russian Grammar:*

Acc.	Accusative case
Adj.	Adjective
Anim.	Animate
Dat.	Dative case
Def.	Definition
Fem.	Feminine gender
Gen.	Genitive case
Impf.	Imperfective aspect
Inf.	Infinitive
Instr.	Instrumental case
Int.	Interrogative
Lit.	Literally
Masc.	Masculine gender
Neut.	Neuter gender
Nom.	Nominative case
Pers.	Person
Pf.	Perfective aspect
Pl.	Plural
Prep.	Prepositional case
Rel.	Relative
Sing.	Singular

PRONUNCIATION

THE RUSSIAN ALPHABET

Learning the sequence of the 33 letters of the Russian alphabet, given here in upper and lower case, will enable you to use a Russian dictionary. Although the italic forms are not employed in the present volume, they are included here for recognition; they are used in Russian books for emphasis and decoration (like our italics), and they are the basis of Russian handwriting, which is essentially a connected form of printed italics.

REGULAR	ITALIC	PRONUNCIATION
А а	*А а*	*a* in f*a*ther, but cut short
Б б	*Б б*	*b* in *b*ed; *p* in s*p*eak at the end of a word or syllable
В в	*В в*	*v* in *v*ote; *f* in *f*ather at the end of a word or syllable
Г г	*Г г*	*g* in *g*oat; *k* in s*k*in at the end of a word or syllable
Д д	*Д д*	*d* in *d*ay; *t* in s*t*ay at the end of a word or syllable
Е е	*Е е*	*ye* in *ye*t
Ё ё	*Ё ё*	*yaw* in *yaw*n
Ж ж	*Ж ж*	*s* in mea*s*ure
З з	*З з*	*z* in *z*eal
И и	*И и*	*ee* in m*ee*t, but cut short
Й й	*Й й*	*y* in bo*y* (this letter is found only in diphthongs; see page 2)
К к	*К к*	*k* in *k*ite
Л л	*Л л*	*l* in *l*et
М м	*М м*	*m* in *m*ap
Н н	*Н н*	*n* in *n*o
О о	*О о*	*aw* in l*aw*, but cut short
П п	*П п*	*p* in *p*et
Р р	*Р р*	like the rolled *r* in Spanish or Italian
С с	*С с*	*s* in *s*et
Т т	*Т т*	*t* in s*t*ay
У у	*У у*	*oo* in f*oo*d, but cut short

1

Ф ф	*Ф ф*	*f* in *f*eed
Х х	*Х х*	like the German *ch* in ho*ch*
Ц ц	*Ц ц*	*ts* in le*ts*
Ч ч	*Ч ч*	*ch* in *ch*air
Ш ш	*Ш ш*	*sh* in *sh*all
Щ щ	*Щ щ*	*shch* in fre*sh ch*eese
Ъ ъ	*Ъ ъ*	the "hard sign" with no distinct sound; indicates the preceding consonant is hard (see next section, "Vowels and Consonants")
Ы ы	*Ы ы*	a short *i*, somewhat as in m*i*lk
Ь ь	*Ь ь*	the "soft sign" with no distinct sound; indicates the preceding consonant is soft (see next section, "Vowels and Consonants")
Э э	*Э э*	*e* in l*e*t
Ю ю	*Ю ю*	like the word *you*
Я я	*Я я*	*ya* in *ya*rd

VOWELS AND CONSONANTS

Russian has 10 vowels: а, е, ё, и, о, у, ы, э, ю and я. The semivowel й occurs only in diphthongs, that is (except in a few words), after another vowel. Although it has no distinct sound of its own, its presence does affect the sounds of the vowels with which it is paired.

DIPHTHONG	PRONUNCIATION
ай	like *ie* in l*ie*
ей	like *ya* in *Ya*le
ой	like *oy* in b*oy*
уй	like *ooey* in ph*ooey* (but pronounced as one syllable)

The pronunciation of the two vowels и and ы is relatively unaffected when they are joined with й to form diphthongs. Thus ий is pronounced much like и, and ый much like ы.

Of the 20 Russian consonants, every one except ч and щ is hard when followed by the vowels а, о, у, ы or э, or when it comes at the end of a word. Most hard consonants are pronounced in a similar way to their English counterparts. With the exception of ж, ц and ш, hard consonants can become soft (or palatalized) when followed either by the vowels е, ё, и, ю or я, or by the soft sign (ь). Soft consonants are pronounced with the middle or forward part of the tongue raised toward the roof of the mouth. The hard sign (ъ) occurs for the most part only after prefixes and before the vowels e, ё, ю and я. It indicates that the preceding consonant is hard.

STRESS

Stress is more emphatic in Russian than in English. In Russian words of more than one syllable, the stress only falls on one syllable. (Throughout the present book the stressed syllable of a word is indicated by an acute accent [´]. It is not normally indicated in writing.) It is important to recognize stress in Russian because it affects the pronunciation of vowels to an even greater extent than in English. A Russian vowel only has its full value in a stressed syllable; it is "reduced" when unstressed. The most important variations in the pronunciation of vowels in stressed syllables, syllables immediately preceding stressed syllables and unstressed syllables are as follows:

VOWEL	STRESSED	PRECEDING STRESS	UNSTRESSED
o	*aw* in l*aw*	*a* in f*a*ther	*e* in th*e*
e	*ye* in *ye*t	*ee* in f*ee*, but cut short	*ee* in f*ee*, but cut short

The vowels y, и and ы are not greatly affected by variations in stress, although they do become somewhat shorter. The soft vowel я reduces from a *ya* to an *uh* sound in unstressed syllables. The soft vowel ё always retains its full value since it occurs only in stressed syllables.

WORD ORDER

The structure and word order of a Russian sentence are often extremely close to those of its English counterpart. For instance, there is a word-to-word correspondence in the following long statement:

Я про́дал то ста́рое си́нее кре́сло, кото́рое я купи́л 25 лет
   наза́д.
I sold that old blue chair that I bought 25 years ago.

Like English, Russian word order can be flexible to show emphasis or shades of meaning (e.g., "I'll go home tomorrow" or "Tomorrow I'll go home"). But Russian can be even more flexible than English because the Russian language has a system of declensions whereby special case endings indicate the role that a word is playing in a sentence. (In English, a more rigid word order tends to indicate the role.)

In two important respects, Russian sentences can be even simpler than their English counterparts: (1) Russian has no articles, definite ("the") or indefinite ("a" or "an"). Thus the sentence Она́ хо́чет купи́ть золо-ты́е часы́ can mean either "She wants to buy *the* gold watch" or "She wants to buy *a* gold watch." In most cases the context of the statement will make the meaning clear. (2) The present tense of the verb "to be" (быть) is almost always omitted.

Весна́ — моё люби́мое вре́мя го́да.
Spring (is) my favorite time of year.

In written Russian, the verb быть is replaced by a dash when separating a subject from a predicate nominative:

Мой оте́ц — врач. Моя́ мать — учи́тельница.
My father (is) a doctor. My mother (is) a teacher.

Note, however, that when the subject is a pronoun the dash is usually omitted: он врач ("he is a doctor"), она́ учи́тельница ("she is a teacher").

"THERE IS," "THERE ARE"

The expression "there is" (or "there are") has two uses in English: (1) to point to the location of an object that is within view (e.g., "There are your glasses"); or (2) to state the existence of something (e.g., "There are tigers in India").

To express the first idea, Russian uses the word вот, which can mean "there," "there is," "there are," "here," "here is," "here are":

Вот мой карандаши́.	*There are* (OR: *Here are*) my pencils.
Вот авто́бус.	*Here's* (OR: *There's*) the bus.

To express the second meaning of "there is" (or "there are"), Russian uses the word есть in positive statements, and the word нет in negative statements:

В ко́мнате **есть** кре́сло.   *There is* an armchair in the room.

В э́том ряду́ **нет** свобо́дных мест.
In this row *there are no* vacant seats.

HOW TO FORM QUESTIONS

There are three chief ways in which to form questions in Russian, all similar to English patterns:

1. Many questions are introduced by interrogative words (but note that the subject and verb are not interchanged as in English):

Когда́ он пришёл?	*When* did he come?
Что он де́лает здесь?	*What* is he doing here?
Куда́ она́ идёт?	*Where* is she going?

The most frequently used interrogative words are: где ("where?"—i.e., "at what place?"); заче́м ("for what purpose?"); как ("how?"); како́й ("what kind?"); когда́ ("when?"); кто ("who?"); куда́ ("where?"— i.e., "to what place?"); отку́да ("from what place?"); почему́ ("why?"); and что ("what?").

2. When no interrogative word is used, the word order of the declarative statement can be retained, and the questioning indicated merely by a different intonation of the sentence, as in English:

Он сего́дня пришёл.	He arrived today.
Он сего́дня пришёл?	He arrived today?

3. When the subject and verb are interchanged as in English, the word ли is inserted after the verb (or other word to be emphasized):

Зна́ет ли он э́то?	Does he know that?
Придёт ли она́?	Is she coming?

This type of question is often used with the negating word не ("not") to form polite requests corresponding to English "won't you," "wouldn't you," "couldn't you," etc.:

Не пойдёте **ли** вы со мной?	*Won't* you go with me?
Не мо́жете **ли** вы нам помо́чь?	*Couldn't* you help us?

NEGATION

The Russian word for "no" is нет. To negate most statements, insert не ("not") before the word to be negated. As in English, this word will usually be the verb.

Я **не** пойду завтра.	I will *not* go tomorrow.
Я **не** сказал ему это.	I did *not* tell him that.

Other elements of a sentence besides the verb can be negated for special emphasis:

Я **не** ему сказал это.	It was *not* to him that I said that.
Это **не** я ему сказал.	It was *not* I who told him that.

Unlike English, which avoids double negatives, Russian keeps the negating particle не even when a sentence is negated by a special negative word (e.g., ничего, "nothing"; никто, "no one"; никогда, "never"; никак, "in no way"):

Я **ничего** не знаю.	I know *nothing*.
Я **никак** не могу.	I can*not in any way*.

NOUNS

GENDER

Russian nouns are either masculine, feminine or neuter in gender. Generally speaking, nouns denoting male persons or animals are masculine in gender, and nouns denoting female persons or animals are feminine in gender. Thus, отéц ("father") and брат ("brother") are masculine; and мать ("mother") and сестрá ("sister") are feminine. The gender of a noun can often be determined from the last letter of the word when in the nominative singular (the dictionary form):

1. All nouns ending in a hard consonant or -й, and many nouns ending in -ь, are masculine in gender: стол ("table"), лес ("forest"), зал ("hall"), герóй ("hero"), учúтель ("teacher"). A few nouns ending in -a or -я and denoting male animate beings are masculine: дя́дя ("uncle"), мужчúна ("man"), дéдушка ("grandfather") and others.

2. Most nouns ending in -a or -я, and all nouns ending in -ия, are feminine: кнúга ("book"), стенá ("wall"), вóдка ("vodka"), жéнщина ("woman"), тётя ("aunt"), фамúлия ("surname"). Many nouns ending in -ь are feminine: дверь ("door"), ночь ("night").

3. Nouns ending in -о or -е are neuter: окнó ("window"), дéрево ("tree"), пóле ("field"), здáние ("building"). All nouns ending in -мя are neuter: врéмя ("time"), úмя ("name"). A few neuter nouns—of non-Russian origin—end in -и or -у: таксú ("taxi"), рагý ("ragout").

CASE

In the English sentence "Peter sees Paul" it is the (unchangeable) word order alone that shows that "Peter" is the subject (the one who is seeing) and "Paul" is the object (the one who is seen). In more complicated English sentences the relationship between nouns is expressed by using prepositions (i.e., "Peter gives the pencil to Paul"). In Russian the relationships between nouns are indicated by the endings of the nouns, no matter what word order is used. The Russian sentences Пётр вúдит Пáвла and Пáвла вúдит

8

Пётр both mean (with slightly different emphasis) "Peter sees Paul" because Пётр ("Peter") is in the nominative case (subject of the verb) and Па́вла ("Paul") is in the accusative case (direct object of the verb). To express "Paul sees Peter," the nouns would be Па́вел and Петра́. Russian uses such case endings to indicate the function of nouns, pronouns and adjectives within a statement. The endings also indicate whether a noun is in the singular or plural: соба́ка ("dog," in the nominative singular), соба́ки ("dogs," in the nominative plural). The part of a noun that generally remains constant is called the stem. For "dog" the stem is собак-. There are six cases in Russian: nominative, accusative, genitive, dative, instrumental and prepositional (or locative).

NOUN DECLENSION

The Nominative Singular

The nominative singular is the dictionary form of the noun. It is used when the noun is the subject of the sentence: соба́ка ла́ет ("*the dog barks*"). The nominative is also used as the so-called predicate nominative in sentences like "Ivan is a professor," in which "Ivan" is the subject nominative and "professor" is the predicate nominative. This type of predicate is in the nominative when "to be" is in the present tense, that is, when this verb is not expressed in Russian: Ива́н — профе́ссор.

The Accusative Singular

Formation of the Accusative. In forming the accusative case, masculine nouns fall into two classes. For masculine nouns denoting inanimate objects (things, abstractions) the accusative form is the same as the nominative: стол, лес. For masculine nouns denoting animate objects (persons and animals) the accusative form takes the ending -a or -я. (Note that when case endings, singular and plural, are added to nouns, the nominative singular endings -й and -ь usually drop away.) Thus Ива́н becomes Ива́на; геро́й becomes геро́я; and учи́тель becomes учи́теля.

Feminine nouns take the accusative ending -y if the nominative form ends in -a, and the ending -ю if the nominative ends in -я. If the nominative ends in -ь, there is no change to form the accusative. Thus стена́ becomes сте́ну; земля́ ("earth") becomes зе́млю; and дверь remains the same. Стена́ and земля́ are examples of feminine nouns that undergo a shift in stress in the accusative. Other common feminines to which this rule applies are страна́ ("country"), рука́ ("hand" or "arm"), нога́ ("foot" or "leg"), вода́ ("water"), зима́ ("winter") and душа́ ("soul").

All neuter nouns remain in exactly the same form in the accusative singular as in the nominative singular: окно́, де́рево, по́ле.

Use of the Accusative. The primary use of the accusative is to indicate that the noun in question is the direct object of the verb:

Сейча́с он чита́ет **Турге́нева.**	Right now he is reading *Turgenev.*
Ива́н ку́рит **папиро́су.**	Ivan is smoking *a cigarette.*
Я ви́жу **де́рево.**	I see *the tree.*

The accusative is also used after the prepositions в ("to, into"; во before certain double consonants) and на ("on, to") when they indicate motion:

Она́ е́дет в **Москву́.**	She is going to *Moscow.*
Мы е́дем на **заво́д.**	We are going to *the factory.*

The Genitive Singular

Formation of the Genitive. Masculine nouns take the genitive ending -a if the nominative form ends in a consonant, and the ending -я if the nominative ends in -й or -ь. Thus стол becomes стола́; лес becomes ле́са; геро́й becomes геро́я; and учи́тель becomes учи́теля.

Feminine nouns take the genitive ending -и when the nominative form ends in -я or -ь, or when the stem ends in г-, к-, х-, ж-, ч-, ш- or щ-. Otherwise the genitive ending is -ы. Thus Со́ня ("Sonia") becomes Со́ни; ночь becomes но́чи; во́дка becomes во́дки; and ко́мната ("room") becomes ко́мнаты.

Neuter nouns take the genitive ending -a when the nominative ends in -о, and the ending -я when the nominative ends in -e. Thus окно́ becomes окна́; де́рево becomes де́рева; and по́ле becomes по́ля.

Use of the Genitive. The primary purpose of the genitive case when used without a preposition is to show possession. The noun that possesses takes the genitive case and is always placed after the noun possessed. Thus, сла́ва геро́я is the only possible Russian form for either "the glory of the hero" or "the hero's glory" in English. "Ivan's field" is по́ле Ива́на.

In general, the Russian genitive construction corresponds to English phrases formed with the preposition "of," even if the relation is not one of possession narrowly understood, but of quality or relation:

кусо́к **хле́ба**	a piece *of bread*
кры́ша **зда́ния**	the roof *of the building*
ка́рта **Аме́рики**	a map *of America*
причи́на **пожа́ра**	the cause *of the fire*

Note, however, that in a phrase like "the city of Moscow," Russian considers the second noun to be in apposition to the first (as if the phrase were "the city Moscow") and thus the second noun will be in the same case as the first.

Another use of the genitive is to convey the meaning "some" or "any" (even if these words are not expressed in English):

| Да́йте ему́ **хле́ба**. | Give him *some bread*. |
| Вы хоти́те **воды́**? | Do you want *any water*? |

Those familiar with French will recognize this as the so-called partitive construction, and quite similar to sentences like "Donnez-lui *du pain*" and "Voulez-vous *de l'eau*?" A few masculine nouns—such as суп ("soup"), сыр ("cheese") and чай ("tea")—take the endings -y or -ю (instead of the normal genitive endings -a or -я) for this partitive use:

| Да́йте ему́ **су́пу**. | Give him *some soup*. |
| Вы хоти́те **ча́ю**? | Do you want *some tea*? |

The genitive is used after words expressing an indefinite quantity such as мно́го ("much" or "many"), ма́ло ("little" or "few"), ско́лько ("how much" or "how many") and не́сколько ("several"). When the meaning is "much" or "little" the genitive singular is used:

Ско́лько **хле́ба** у вас?
How much *bread* do you have?

В се́верной А́фрике о́чень ма́ло **воды́**.
In northern Africa there is very little *water*.

The direct object (which is normally in the accusative case) often takes the genitive case in constructions in which the verb is negated. This occurs especially when the direct object is abstract or refers to an entire class of things rather than to a specific object or person:

| Мы не хоти́м **войны́**. | We don't want *war*. |
| Я не пью **ча́я**. Я не ем **сы́ра**. | I don't drink *tea*. I don't eat *cheese*. |

There are a number of important verbs that govern the genitive case. These include добива́ться ("to strive for"), жа́ждать ("to crave for"), жела́ть ("to desire"), заслу́живать ("to deserve") and достига́ть ("to achieve").

The genitive is also used with a number of prepositions (see page 43) and after numerals (see page 90).

The Dative Singular

Formation of the Dative. Masculine nouns take the dative ending -ю when their nominative form ends in -й or -ь; otherwise, masculine nouns add the ending -y to form the dative. Thus герой becomes герою; учитель becomes учителю; and Иван becomes Ивану.

Feminine nouns with the nominative endings -a or -я change these endings to -e to form the dative. Feminines ending in -ь in the nominative take the dative ending -и. Those ending in -ия in the nominative change the ending to -ии to form the dative. Thus книга becomes книге; Соня becomes Соне; дверь becomes двери; and партия ("party," in the political sense) becomes партии.

Neuter nouns with the nominative ending -o change this to -y to form the dative; neuters with the nominative ending -e change this to -ю. Thus дерево becomes дереву; and поле becomes полю.

Use of the Dative. The basic use of the dative (when used without a preposition) is to indicate the indirect object. This rule generally applies when the indirect object is a person:

Я дал книгу **Ивану**.	I gave the book *to Ivan*.
Кто продал **Сергею** эту машину?	Who sold *Sergei* that car?

Каждый месяц Наташа пишет **Тамаре**.
Every month Natasha writes *to Tamara*.

The dative case is also often used in impersonal constructions: Ивану холодно ("Ivan is cold"); Соне жарко ("Sonia is hot").

Some transitive verbs take a direct object (usually in the accusative) in the dative. The most common such verbs are помогать ("to help"), мешать ("to hinder"), советовать ("to advise"), вредить ("to harm"), напоминать ("to remind"), повиноваться ("to obey"), позволять ("to allow"), служить ("to serve"), верить ("to believe") and завидовать ("to envy"):

Кто помогает Ивану? Who is helping Ivan?

Иван мешает Соне читать.
Ivan is preventing Sonia from reading.

The dative is also used after certain prepositions (see page 44). Note that nouns that do not denote persons usually require a preposition when they are in the dative.

The Instrumental Singular

Formation of the Instrumental. Masculine nouns take the instrumental ending -ем (or -ём if the ending receives the stress) when the nominative ends in -й or -ь. Those masculine nouns ending in -ж, -ц, -ч, -ш or -щ in the nominative take the ending -ом if the stress is on the last syllable and -ем if it is not. All other masculine nouns take the ending -ом. Thus герой becomes героем; учитель becomes учителем; словарь ("dictionary") becomes словарём; нож ("knife") becomes ножом; товарищ ("comrade") becomes товарищем; and стол becomes столом.

Feminine nouns ending in -a in the nominative take the ending -ой (or, rarely, -ою) to form the instrumental unless the stem ends in ж-, ц-, ч-, ш- or щ-, in which case the instrumental ending is -ей (or -ею). Feminine nouns ending in -я in the nominative take the ending -ей (or -ею) or -ёй (when the ending receives the stress). Feminine nouns ending in -ь in the nominative add the ending -ью to form the instrumental. Thus водка becomes водкой; птица ("bird") becomes птицей; Соня becomes Соней; земля becomes землёй; and осень ("autumn") becomes осенью.

Neuter nouns take the instrumental ending -ом if the nominative ends in -о; the ending -ем if the nominative ends in -е; and the ending -ём if the nominative ends in -ё. Thus окно ("window") becomes окном; поле becomes полем; and ружьё ("gun") becomes ружьём.

Use of the Instrumental. The primary use of the instrumental case (without a preposition) is to indicate the instrument or means by which some action is performed:

Мы поехали туда **машиной**.   We went there *by car*.

Учитель пишет на доске **мелом**.
The teacher writes on the board *with chalk*.

Он говорит **шёпотом**.   He speaks *in a whisper*.

Они вернулись домой **полем**.
They returned home *by way of the field*.

The complement of the verb быть ("to be"), when that verb is in the past or future tense, often takes the instrumental case:

Он был **меха́ником**.	He was *a mechanic*.
Я бу́ду **до́ктором**.	I will be *a doctor*.

When the verb быть is used in the past tense to indicate a permanent condition, however, the nominative rather than the instrumental is used. Compare these two sentences:

Пу́шкин был студе́нтом.	Pushkin was a student. [Temporary]
Пу́шкин был ру́сский.	Pushkin was a Russian. [Permanent]

Certain Russian verbs are always followed by the instrumental, irrespective of the tense. These include де́латься ("to become"), служи́ть ("to serve [as]"), занима́ться ("to study"), интересова́ться ("to be interested in") and по́льзоваться ("to make use of"):

Э́то мо́жет служи́ть хоро́шим **приме́ром**.
This can serve *as a* good *example*.

Мой брат занима́ется **грамма́тикой**.
My brother is studying *grammar*.

The instrumental case is also used after certain prepositions (see page 44).

The Prepositional Singular

The prepositional case is so called because it must always be introduced by a preposition. The most common prepositions used with this case are в ("in, at"), на ("on, at") and о ("about, concerning"). When о is followed by a word beginning with a vowel it becomes об; thus: о Со́не ("about Sonia"); об Аме́рике ("about America"). When в and о are followed by words that begin with two or more consonants, they become во and о́бо, respectively.

Formation of the Prepositional. Masculine nouns take the ending -e to form the prepositional. Thus стол becomes столе́; геро́й becomes герое́; and слова́рь becomes словаре́. A small but important group of masculine nouns, mostly monosyllabic ones, take the ending -y in the prepositional case after the prepositions в and на. Note that this -y ending is always stressed. This group of nouns includes пол ("floor"), бе́рег ("shore"), мост ("bridge"), сад ("garden"), лес ("forest"), год ("year"), у́гол ("corner"), глаз ("eye"), час ("hour"), шкаф ("cupboard") and рот ("mouth"). Thus:

на полу́	on the floor	в саду́	in the garden
на берегу́	on the shore	в лесу́	in the forest
на мосту́	on the bridge	в году́	in the year
на углу́	at the corner	во рту́	in the mouth

All these masculine nouns take the normal -e ending after the preposition o ("about, concerning"): о по́ле ("about the floor"); о саде́ ("about the garden").

Feminine nouns with nominatives ending in -a or -я take the ending -e in the prepositional. Feminines with nominatives ending in -ия, however, take the ending -ии; those with nominatives ending in -ь take the ending -и. (The prepositions given in the following examples are to show usage—different prepositions could be used.) Thus ко́мната becomes в ко́мнате ("in the room"); Со́ня becomes о Со́не ("about Sonia"); па́ртия becomes о па́ртии ("about the party"); and дверь becomes о две́ри ("about the door").

Neuter nouns with the nominative ending in -o take the ending -e in the prepositional. Neuter nouns with the nominative ending in a consonant plus -e remain unchanged for the prepositional case; those with nominatives ending in -ие, however, take the ending -ии. (In the following examples the prepositions о and в are used to show that a noun in the prepositional case must always appear with a preposition, not necessarily о or в.) Thus де́рево becomes о де́реве ("about the tree"); по́ле becomes о по́ле ("about the field"); and зда́ние becomes в зда́нии ("in the building").

Use of the Prepositional. Examples of the prepositional case used with the prepositions о (об), в (во) and на:

Ле́кция была́ **о Пу́шкине**.	The lecture was *about Pushkin*.
Она́ **в ко́мнате**.	She is *in the room*.
Кни́га лежи́т **на столе́**.	The book is lying *on the table*.

NOUN PLURALS

The plural forms of nouns are in general simpler to learn than the singular.

The Nominative Plural

Most masculine nouns take the ending -ы or -и in the nominative plural. They take the ending -и instead of -ы when the nominative singular ends in

-й or -ь, or in -г, -ж, -к, -х, -ч, -ш or -щ. Thus стол becomes столы́ ("tables"); геро́й becomes геро́и ("heroes"); автомоби́ль becomes автомоби́ли ("cars"); and това́рищ becomes това́рищи ("comrades"). Some masculine nouns take the nominative plural ending -a or -я (-я if the nominative singular ends in -ь). This group includes some very common words (note that their plural ending is always stressed):

глаз/глаза́	eye/eyes
го́лос/голоса́	voice/voices
го́род/города́	city/cities
до́ктор/доктора́	doctor/doctors
дом/дома́	house/houses
по́езд/поезда́	train/trains
профе́ссор/профессора́	professor/professors
учи́тель/учителя́	teacher/teachers

Feminine nouns take the ending -ы or -и in the nominative plural. They take the ending -и instead of -ы when the nominative singular ends in -я or -ь, or when the stem ends in г-, ж-, к-, х-, ч-, ш- or щ-. Thus пти́ца becomes пти́цы ("birds"); па́ртия becomes па́ртии ("parties"); дверь becomes две́ри ("doors"); and кни́га becomes кни́ги ("books").

Neuter nouns take the ending -a in the nominative plural if the nominative singular ends in -o; -я if it ends in -e (except that those neuters ending in -же, -це, -че, -ше or -ще in the singular take the ending -a in the plural). A few neuters take the nominative plural ending -и. Thus окно́ becomes о́кна ("windows"); по́ле becomes поля́ ("fields"); се́рдце ("heart") becomes сердца́ ("hearts"); and я́блоко ("apple") becomes я́блоки ("apples").

A large number of feminine and neuter nouns have a stress in the nominative plural that differs from that in the singular. (When the vowel e is involved, an e/ё alternation sometimes occurs.) This change in stress often serves to differentiate the nominative plural from the genitive singular in spoken Russian:

NOM. SING.	GEN. SING.	NOM. PL.
стена́	стены́	сте́ны
жена́	жены́	жёны
по́ле	поля́	поля́

The Accusative Plural

For inanimate masculine nouns, the accusative plural is exactly like the nominative plural. Thus стол becomes столы́. For animate masculines (persons and animals), the accusative plural is the same as the genitive plural (see next section).

The accusative plural of inanimate feminine nouns is like the nominative plural. Thus дверь becomes двéри. For animate feminines, the accusative plural is the same as the genitive plural (see next section).

Inanimate neuters in the accusative plural are exactly like the nominative plural. Thus окнó becomes óкна; пóле becomes поля́; сéрдце becomes сердца́; and я́блоко becomes я́блоки. The accusative plural of animate neuters is the same as the genitive plural (see next section).

The Genitive Plural

Masculine nouns generally take the ending -ов in the genitive plural. However, they take the ending -ев if the nominative singular ends in -й or in -ц (if the stress is on the preceding syllable). They take the ending -ей if the nominative singular ends in -ь or in -ж, -ч, -ш or -щ. Thus стол becomes столóв; герóй becomes герóев; мéсяц becomes мéсяцев; учи́тель becomes учителéй; and товáрищ becomes товáрищей.

The most common feminine nouns—those ending in -a in the nominative singular—take no ending in the genitive plural. Thus стенá becomes стен; кни́га becomes книг. Those feminines that end in -ь in the nominative singular take the ending -ей in the genitive plural: дверь becomes дверéй. Those that end in -я preceded by a consonant in the nominative singular take the ending -ь in the genitive plural. Thus недéля ("week") becomes недéль. Those that end in -я preceded by a vowel in the nominative singular take the ending -й in the genitive plural. Thus пáртия becomes пáртий. When the stem ends in a consonant cluster, a vowel is often inserted between the consonants in the genitive plural. Thus бáбушка ("grandmother") becomes бáбушек; сестрá becomes сестёр; and земля́ becomes земéль.

Neuter nouns that end in -о in the nominative singular take no ending in the genitive plural: мéсто ("place") becomes мест. Here again, a vowel is often inserted between final consonants: окнó becomes óкон. Neuters that end in -е (but not -ие) in the nominative singular take the ending -ей in the genitive plural: пóле becomes полéй. Those that end in -ие in the nominative singular take the ending -ий in the genitive plural: здáние becomes здáний.

The Dative Plural

In the dative plural, all nouns end in -ам or -ям. The -ям ending is taken by (1) masculine nouns with nominative singulars ending in -й or -ь; (2) feminine nouns with nominative singulars ending in -я or -ь; and (3) neuter nouns with nominative singulars ending in -е. Thus стол becomes столáм; герóй becomes герóям; учи́тель becomes учи́телям; стенá becomes стенáм; Сóня becomes Сóням; часть becomes частя́м; окнó becomes óкнам; and пóле becomes поля́м.

The Instrumental Plural

In the instrumental plural, nouns take the ending -ами or -ями. The -ями ending is taken by those nouns that take the -ям ending in the dative plural. Thus стол becomes столáми; герóй becomes герóями, etc.

The Prepositional Plural

In the prepositional plural, nouns take the ending -ах or -ях. The -ях ending is taken by those nouns that take the -ям ending in the dative case and the -ями ending in the instrumental case. Thus стол becomes столáх; герóй becomes герóях, etc.

SPECIAL NOUN DECLENSIONS AND IRREGULAR NOUNS

There are a number of special noun declensions and irregular nouns that do not fall into any of the patterns given thus far. The most important of these subdeclensions and irregularities are shown in Appendix I: Special Noun Declensions and Irregular Nouns (page 87).

COLLECTIVE NOUNS AND NOUNS WITH ONLY SINGULAR OR ONLY PLURAL FORMS

1. Like English, Russian has a fairly large number of collective nouns, nouns that are grammatically singular although they refer to a group or class: толпá ("crowd"), нарóд ("nation, people," as in "the Chinese people"), молодёжь ("young people, youth," as in "the youth of our cities"). Many such nouns in Russian refer to produce: лук ("onions"), картóфель ("potatoes"), горóх ("peas"), etc.

2. A number of Russian nouns have plural forms only. Sometimes the plural meaning is obvious and there is an English equivalent: брю́ки ("trousers"), но́жницы ("scissors"), очки́ ("spectacles"). Some other important plural-only nouns are де́ньги ("money"), воро́та ("gate"), сли́вки ("cream"), часы́ ("watch"), са́ни ("sled"). The accusative, dative and instrumental of these words presents no problem; you will only need to learn the way in which they form the genitive. The genitive of the words listed above: брюк, но́жниц, очко́в, де́нег, воро́т, сли́вок, часо́в, сане́й.

3. Two important plural-only nouns, де́ти ("children, babies") and лю́ди ("people," not in the political sense), have equivalents in the singular that are completely different words. Де́ти (ACC. дете́й, GEN. дете́й, DAT. де́тям, INSTR. детьми́, PREP. де́тях) has the singular-number equivalent ребёнок ("child, baby"). Лю́ди (ACC. люде́й, GEN. люде́й, DAT. лю́дям, INSTR. людьми́, PREP. лю́дях) has the singular-number equivalent челове́к ("person, human being").

ADJECTIVES

AGREEMENT OF ADJECTIVES WITH NOUNS

Russian adjectives, like their English equivalents, may precede the noun they modify (e.g., "the tall man," "the blue car") or be linked to it by a verb (e.g., "the man is tall," "the car was blue"). Unlike English adjectives, however, Russian adjectives must agree in gender, number (i.e., singular or plural) and case with the nouns they modify.

FORMS OF ADJECTIVES

Hard Adjectives

Most adjectives end in -ый in the masculine nominative singular (the dictionary form for adjectives). Such adjectives are known as hard adjectives. For these adjectives the full declension is as follows (using the model word нóвый, "new"):

	SINGULAR			PLURAL
	MASC.	FEM.	NEUT.	ALL GENDERS
NOM.	нóвый	нóвая	нóвое	нóвые
ACC.	нóвый	нóвую	нóвое	нóвые
(ANIM.)	нóвого			нóвых
GEN.	нóвого	нóвой	нóвого	нóвых
DAT.	нóвому	нóвой	нóвому	нóвым
INSTR.	нóвым	нóвой	нóвым	нóвыми
PREP.	нóвом	нóвой	нóвом	нóвых

1. If they modify animate nouns, masculine adjectives in the accusative singular, and adjectives of all genders in the accusative plural, have the same form as the genitive rather than the form of the nominative.

2. The letter г in the masculine and neuter genitive singular ending is pronounced like English *v*.

20

3. The feminine instrumental singular also possesses the old-fashioned ending -ою (as in но́вою), which appears in older literature.

4. When the stress falls on the last syllable of this class of adjectives, the masculine singular nominative (and inanimate accusative) has the ending -о́й instead of -ый. Thus: больно́й ("ill"), голубо́й ("light blue"), молодо́й ("young"). All the other forms of such adjectives are as shown above.

5. When the stem ends in г-, к- or х-, the ы of the endings is replaced by и. Thus, the adjective ру́сский ("Russian") has the masculine and neuter instrumental ру́сским and the plural forms: NOM. ру́сские, ACC. ру́сские, GEN. ру́сских, DAT. ру́сским, INSTR. ру́сскими, PREP. ру́сских.

6. When the stem ends in ж-, ч-, ш- or щ-, the ы of the endings is replaced by и, and the о (when not stressed) is replaced by е. (Note that only the first о in the ending -ого is replaced.) Thus, in the case of све́жий ("fresh"), the nominative and accusative neuter is све́жее; the genitive forms are: MASC. & NEUT. све́жего, FEM. све́жей; the dative forms are: MASC. & NEUT. све́жему, FEM. све́жей; the feminine instrumental is све́жей (or све́жею); and the prepositional forms are: MASC. & NEUT. све́жем, FEM. све́жей.

Soft Adjectives

The adjective declension discussed above is the so-called hard declension. The important secondary declension is known as the soft declension. In the soft declension the masculine nominative singular always ends in -ий, and the endings never bear the stress. The declension for soft adjectives is as follows (using the model word си́ний, "dark blue"):

	SINGULAR			PLURAL
	MASC.	FEM.	NEUT.	ALL GENDERS
NOM.	си́ний	си́няя	си́нее	си́ние
ACC.	си́ний	си́нюю	си́нее	си́ние
(ANIM.)	си́него			си́них
GEN.	си́него	си́ней	си́него	си́них
DAT.	си́нему	си́ней	си́нему	си́ним
INSTR.	си́ним	си́ней	си́ним	си́ними
PREP.	си́нем	си́ней	си́нем	си́них

The feminine instrumental singular has an alternate ending -ею (си́нею).

The possessive adjectives мой ("my"), твой ("your"), etc., and a number of other adjectives that partake of the nature of pronouns are discussed in the chapter on pronouns (see page 34).

USE OF ADJECTIVES

1. The following sentences demonstrate the agreement of adjectives with nouns:

Я ви́дел **чёрного** быка́ и **бе́лую** коро́ву в по́ле.
I saw a *black* bull and a *white* cow in the field.
(dictionary forms: чёрный, here masc. acc. sing. animate, modifying быка́; and бе́лый, here fem. acc. sing., modifying коро́ву)

Де́ти игра́ют во дворе́ **ста́рого** до́ма.
The children are playing in the yard of the *old* house.
(dictionary form: ста́рый, here masc. gen. sing., modifying до́ма)

Официа́нт по́дал счёт **скупо́му** дя́де Серге́ю.
The waiter gave the check to *stingy* Uncle Sergei.
(dictionary form: скупо́й, here masc. dat. sing., modifying дя́де)

Учи́тель пи́шет **жёлтым** ме́лом.
The teacher writes with *yellow* chalk.
(dictionary form: жёлтый, here masc. instr. sing., modifying ме́лом)

Конто́ра Петра́ в **кирпи́чном** зда́нии на **обра́тной** стороне́ у́лицы.
Peter's office is in a *brick* building on the *opposite* side of the street.
(dictionary forms: кирпи́чный, here neut. prep. sing., modifying зда́нии; and обра́тный, here fem. prep. sing., modifying стороне́)

У нас сего́дня нет **све́жих** фру́ктов.
We have no *fresh* fruit today.
(dictionary form: све́жий, here masc. gen. pl., modifying фру́ктов)

Укра́сили зал **я́ркими** цвета́ми.
The hall has been decorated with *bright* flowers.
(dictionary form: я́ркий, here masc. instr. pl., modifying цвета́ми)

2. Russian adjectives can often be used as substantives—that is, as subjects or objects of a verb on their own account, with no noun expressed. Compare these two sentences:

Больна́я де́вушка кри́кнула.   The *sick* girl cried out.

Больна́я кри́кнула.
The sick woman (OR: *woman patient*) cried out.

Thus, скупо́й can mean "a miser" as well as "miserly"; ни́щий can mean "a beggar" as well as "beggarly"; etc.

3. Aside from the above kind of substantive use of adjectives, there are several adjectives that for all practical purposes have become nouns, but are still declined like adjectives. Some are masculine, e.g., рабо́чий ("worker"), пле́нный ("prisoner"), портно́й ("tailor"); GEN. SING. рабо́чего, пле́нного, портно́го. Others, including many names of rooms and shops, are feminine, e.g., гости́ная ("living room"), ва́нная ("bathroom"), столо́вая ("dining room"), бу́лочная ("bakery"), парикма́херская ("barber shop"), мастерска́я ("workshop, studio"); GEN. SING. гости́ной, ва́нной, столо́вой, бу́лочной, etc.

SHORT FORMS OF ADJECTIVES

Formation of the Short Form

So far (if we momentarily disregard the independent use of adjectives as nouns) we have been discussing only adjectives that immediately precede the nouns they modify; this is known as the attributive use of adjectives. But in Russian as in English, adjectives can occur in the predicate after verbs of being: "That book is *useful*," "These flowers are *beautiful*," etc. When used predicatively, many Russian adjectives (but never those declined like си́ний) have an optional short form, which naturally exists in the nominative only.

The masculine singular short form is the stem alone; the feminine singular short form ends in -a; the neuter in -o; and the plural for all genders in -ы (or -и if the stem ends in г-, к-, х-, ж-, ч-, ш- or щ-). Thus, the short forms for краси́вый ("beautiful") are краси́в, краси́ва, краси́во, краси́вы.

When consonants fall together at the end of the stem, a vowel (o, e or ё) is inserted in the masculine short form. Thus, the short forms of интере́сный ("interesting"), злой ("evil") and у́мный ("intelligent") are:

MASCULINE	FEMININE	NEUTER	PLURAL
интере́сен	интере́сна	интере́сно	интере́сны
зол	зла	зло	злы
умён	умна́	умно́	умны́

The last example shows that stress is liable to shift in the short form.

Use of the Short Form

1. In modern spoken Russian, the long form is preferred in the predicate when there is a choice. But in some instances the short form must be used. In general, when a distinction is made, the long form denotes a permanent or intrinsic condition, and the short form denotes a transitory or qualified condition. Compare the following pairs of sentences:

Он о́чень **спосо́бный**.
He is very *talented*. [In general]

Он о́чень **спосо́бен** к языка́м.
He is very *good* at languages. [A qualified, limited talent]

Её оте́ц **занято́й** челове́к.	Her father is a *busy* man.
Её оте́ц **за́нят**.	Her father is *busy at the moment*.

2. Some predicative adjectives have different meanings depending on whether they are in the long or the short form. Thus, in the predicate, пра́вый means "right" as opposed to "left," whereas прав, права́ means "right" as opposed to "wrong." The long form of живо́й means "lively"; the short form жив, жива́ means "alive."

3. Some adjectives are so descriptive of a momentary situation that they are usually in the short form when used predicatively. Examples (given here in the short form): дово́лен ("satisfied"), благода́рен ("grateful"), уве́рен ("sure, certain"), го́лоден ("hungry"), сча́стлив ("happy, lucky"), гото́в ("ready"), наме́рен ("of a mind to"), до́лжен ("obliged, under the necessity of"):

Я **наме́рен** пойти́ с ва́ми.	I *intend* to go with you.
Вы **должны́** пойти́ со мной.	You *must* go with me.

4. The adjective рад ("glad") has only short forms: рад, ра́да, ра́до, ра́ды.

5. One special use of the short form, with adjectives like вели́кий ("big") and ма́лый ("small"), is to denote an excess. Thus:

Э́ти боти́нки мне **велики́**.	These shoes are *too big* for me.
Э́та ко́мната **мала́**.	This room is *too small*.

Note that the words большо́й and ма́ленький, the normal attributive adjectives for "big" and "small," respectively, have no short forms.

COMPARISON OF ADJECTIVES: THE COMPARATIVE

Formation of the Comparative

1. When an adjective is used attributively, its comparative degree is formed by placing the unchangeable adverb бóлее ("more") just before it. Thus: **бóлее красѝвый** дом ("a *more beautiful* house"); **бóлее красѝвые** домá (*"more beautiful* houses"). To express "less," place the unchangeable adverb мéнее before the adjective: **мéнее красѝвый** дом ("a *less beautiful* house"); **мéнее красѝвые** домá (*"less beautiful* houses").

2. When an adjective is used without a noun in the predicate after the verb "to be" (even when this verb is not expressed in the Russian), the comparative form with бóлее may be used. However, unless the adjective is extremely long, it is more acceptable to form its comparative by dropping its ending and adding the unchangeable ending -ee. Thus, э́тот дом красѝвее is preferable to э́тот дом бóлее красѝвый to express "this house is more beautiful."

With few exceptions, the word stress in the -ee comparative form is on the ending if the adjective has a stem of one or two syllables; otherwise, the stress is the same as in the positive: умнéе ("more intelligent"), интерéснее ("more interesting").

3. A considerable number of frequently used adjectives have special predicate comparative forms that display *consonant mutation*. Some of the most common adjectives of this type are:

POSITIVE	COMPARATIVE
блѝзкий ("near")	блѝже ("nearer")
высóкий ("high, tall")	вы́ше ("higher, taller")
глубóкий ("deep")	глу́бже ("deeper")
далёкий ("distant")	дáльше ("more distant")
дóлгий ("long," in time)	дóльше ("longer")
дорогóй ("dear, expensive")	дорóже ("dearer")
мя́гкий ("soft")	мя́гче ("softer")
тѝхий ("quiet")	тѝше ("quieter")
широ́кий ("wide")	шѝре ("wider")

The adjective стáрый ("old") has the regular comparative старéе when referring to things and the special comparative стáрше when referring to people. Some comparative forms are more irregular than those listed above:

POSITIVE	COMPARATIVE
хоро́ший ("good")	лу́чше ("better")
плохо́й ("bad")	ху́же ("worse")

The word бо́льше ("bigger, more") serves as the comparative form of мно́го ("much, many") as well as that of большо́й ("big"). Similarly, ме́ньше ("smaller, less") is the comparative form of both ма́ло ("little, few") and ма́ленький ("small").

Some types of adjectives cannot form comparatives with -ee; these include adjectives ending in -ский, -аный and -яный.

4. A few adjectives in the comparative degree have their own attributive form (in addition to the form with бо́лее): лу́чший ("better"), ху́дший ("worse"), ста́рший ("elder," of persons), мла́дший ("younger," of persons), бо́льший ("bigger"), ме́ньший ("smaller"). Thus, "the better student" can be expressed in two ways: бо́лее хоро́ший студе́нт or лу́чший студе́нт. With the exception of бо́льший and ме́ньший, the above comparatives are really superlatives ("best," "worst," "eldest," etc.) that can be used as attributive comparatives.

Use of the Comparative

1. In Russian the object of comparison (i.e., "B" in the expression "A is bigger than B") is either placed in the genitive case or introduced by the conjunction чем (preceded by a comma). In some instances, either construction can be used. Thus:

Во́лга длинне́е **Невы́**.	The Volga is longer *than the Neva.*
Па́вел лени́вее **Петра́**.	Paul is lazier *than Peter.*
Во́лга длинне́е, **чем** Нева́.	The Volga is longer *than* the Neva.
Па́вел лени́вее, **чем** Пётр.	Paul is lazier *than* Peter.

The construction with чем must be used, however, when the objects compared are not in the nominative case:

Я люблю́ во́ду бо́льше, чем во́дку.
I like water more than vodka.

Here во́дку is in the accusative case just as во́ду is, since both these nouns are direct objects of люблю́. Also compare the two sentences:

Я люблю́ Тама́ру бо́льше, чем **Ли́за**.
I like Tamara more than *Liza does.*

Я люблю Тамару **бо́льше**, чем **Ли́зу**.
I like Tamara more than (*I like*) *Liza*.

2. The comparative degree is frequently used with various prefixes and adverbs in standard expressions:

Са́ша **поста́рше**, чем Ко́ля.   Sasha is *a little* older than Kolya.

Его́ рабо́та стано́вилась **всё ле́гче**.
His work became *easier and easier*.

Ваш дом большо́й, но наш **ещё бо́льше**.
Your house is big, but ours is bigger *still*.

Иди́те сюда́ **как мо́жно скоре́е**.
Come here *as soon as possible*.

Чем бо́льше, **тем** лу́чше.   *The* more *the* better.

Бы́ло **гора́здо** бо́льше люде́й, чем я ожида́л.
There were *many* more people than I expected.

The adverb гора́здо may be used to express "much" or "many" with a comparative; it has no other use.

THE SUPERLATIVE DEGREE

There are two ways in which to form the superlative degree (e.g., "biggest," "most beautiful") in Russian. These are the compound superlative and the suffixal superlative:

1. In formal Russian, the compound superlative is formed by placing the unchangeable adverb наибо́лее ("most") in front of the positive long form of the adjective:

Ми́ша **наибо́лее у́мный** ма́льчик в кла́ссе.
Misha is *the most intelligent* boy in the class.

In colloquial speech, however, it is more common for the positive form of the adjective to be preceded by са́мый ("most"):

Ми́ша **са́мый у́мный** ма́льчик в кла́ссе.
Misha is *the most intelligent* boy in the class.

Unlike наибо́лее, however, са́мый is an adjective, and must agree in gender, number and case with the adjective it precedes. Thus:

О́льга **са́мая у́мная** де́вушка среди́ студе́нтов.
Olga is *the most intelligent* girl among the students.

Он один из **са́мых ужа́сных** тира́нов в исто́рии.
He is one of *the most terrible* tyrants in history.

There are four basic ways in which to express the entire group among which the superlative stands out:

(a) With the genitive:

Он са́мый у́мный студе́нт **кла́сса**.
He is the smartest student *of the class*.

(b) With the preposition в and the prepositional:

Он са́мый у́мный **в кла́ссе**.
He is the smartest *in the class*.

(c) With the preposition из ("out of"; и́зо before double consonants) and the genitive plural:

Он са́мый у́мный **и́зо всех студе́нтов**.
He is the smartest (*out*) *of all the students*.

(d) With the preposition среди́ ("among") and the genitive plural:

Он са́мый у́мный **среди́ студе́нтов**.
He is the smartest *among* (OR: *of*) *the students*.

2. A number of Russian adjectives possess another superlative form that is not generally used to make an actual comparison, but to intensify the meaning of the adjective (e.g., "a most beautiful house," "an extremely beautiful house"). This is the so-called absolute superlative. It is formed by adding the suffix -ейший to the stem of the adjective. Unlike -ee, this suffix is a fully declinable form. Thus: краси́вейший дом ("a most beautiful house"); краси́вейшая де́вушка ("an extremely beautiful girl").

Consonant mutation sometimes occurs in the adjectival stem. When the mutated stem ends in ж-, ч-, ш- or щ-, the ending becomes -айший and is always stressed. Thus высо́кий ("high, tall") becomes высоча́йший ("very high, very tall").

ADVERBS

ADVERBS DERIVED FROM ADJECTIVES

In English, many adverbs are formed by adding -ly to an adjective: quiet, quietly; swift, swiftly. In Russian, adverbs can be formed by adding -o or -e to the stem of adjectives. (Thus adverbs derived from adjectives have the same form as the neuter short form of the adjective.) For hard adjectives, the ending -o is added:

ADJECTIVE	ADVERB IN -o
быстрый ("quick")	быстро ("quickly")
красивый ("beautiful")	красиво ("beautifully")

For soft adjectives, the ending -e is added to the stem to form the adverb:

ADJECTIVE	ADVERB IN -e
искренний ("sincere")	искренне ("sincerely")
крайний ("extreme")	крайне ("extremely")

Adjectives ending in -ский have the adverbial ending -и: технический ("technical"), технически ("technically").

COMPARISON OF ADVERBS

The comparative degree of adverbs formed from adjectives is exactly like the comparative of the adjectives themselves. Thus: умнее ("more intelligent, more intelligently"); глубже ("deeper, more deeply").

To form the superlative degree of adverbs, either add наиболее before the positive degree, or add a genitive form of the pronoun/adjective весь after the comparative degree: наиболее логически ("most logically"); мы знаем **лучше всего** историю ("we know history *best*").

OTHER ADVERBS

Like English, Russian has numerous independent adverbs that are not formed from adjectives (English examples: "now," "there," "onward," "once"). Most Russian adverbs of this type are unchangeable in form and their use in sentences is basically the same as for English adverbs; they come not so much under the category of grammar as that of vocabulary to be learned. Therefore only a few basic notions and a small number of examples will be given here.

Adverbs of Time

Adverbs of time include such words as когда ("when?"), тогда ("then, at that time"), никогда ("never"), сейчас ("now"), сегодня* ("today"), наконец ("finally"), опять ("again"), уже ("already").

Когда and тогда exemplify the frequent pairing in Russian of interrogative words beginning with к- and demonstratives beginning with т-. Когда, like other interrogatives, can be turned into an indefinite by adding -то or -нибудь: когда-то ("at some time"). The adverb никогда is an example of a negative formed from an interrogative through the addition of the prefix ни-.

Adverbs of Place

Adverbs of place fall into two main categories: those of position, or "place in which," and those indicating direction or change in location, "place to or from which." It is important, for example, to distinguish between где and куда, both of which can be translated as "where?"; где means "in which place?" and куда means "to which place?" Both здесь and сюда can be translated as "here"; здесь means "in this place" and сюда means "to this place." Там means "there, in that place"; туда means "there, to that place."

When preceded by не, the demonstrative adverbs там and туда mean "in the wrong place" and "to the wrong place," respectively.

---

* The -г- in сегодня is pronounced like English *v* because it is historically part of the genitive singular ending -его.

Adverbs of Degree

Adverbs of degree include óчень ("very"), мнóго ("much, many, a lot"), мáло ("little, few"), совсéм ("completely"), почтú ("almost"), слúшком ("too, too much").

With verbs of wanting and liking, óчень is used alone to mean "very much": Сóня **óчень** любит цветы́ ("Sonia loves flowers *very much*"). Otherwise мнóго is used: он **мнóго** рабóтает ("he works *a lot*"). Of course, óчень can still modify мнóго in such cases: он **óчень мнóго** рабóтает ("he works *very hard*"). Мнóго and мáло also serve as adverbs of quantity; as such they are discussed in the next section.

Adverbs of Quantity

The words мнóго ("much, many"), немнóго ("a little, a few"), мáло ("little, few"), скóлько ("how much, how many?"), стóлько ("so much, so many") and нéсколько ("somewhat, several") can all be used as pure adverbs, but they can also function as pronouns or adjectives.

They are used with the genitive singular of nouns and pronouns to express amount, and with the genitive plural to express number: мнóго хлéба ("a lot of bread"), немнóго людéй ("a few people"), мáло воды́ ("little water"), скóлько друзéй ("how many friends?"), стóлько врéмени ("so much time"), нéсколько товáрищей ("several comrades").

When followed by singular nouns, these quantity words occur only in the nominative and accusative. When followed by plural nouns, they can occur in the other cases as well; when used in the genitive, dative, instrumental or prepositional, they become adjectives taking the appropriate plural endings:

У **немнóгих** студéнтов бы́ли жáлобы.
A few students had complaints.

Мнóгим людям дáли хлеб бесплáтно.
Many people were given bread free of charge.

Related to мнóго is the regularly declined plural-only adjective мнóгие (it can also be used as a pronoun), which means "many" with an emphasis on the individuals composing the group:

Мнóгие из нóвых студéнтов бы́ли совсéм незнакóмы мне.
Many of the new students were completely unfamiliar to me.

Miscellaneous Adverbs

1. Adverbs of manner include как ("how?"), так ("thus, in this way") and
никáк ("in no way").

2. Тóже and тáкже both mean "also, too, as well," but тóже
introduces a new subject while the predicate stays the same, and тáкже
introduces a new predicate while the subject stays the same:

Михайл рабóтает режиссёром; Борúс, **тóже**.
Mikhail is a film director; Boris is, *too*.

Михайл рабóтает режиссёром. Он **тáкже** пúшет.
Mikhail is a film director. He writes, *too*.

3. The instrumental case of certain nouns is used adverbially. Among them
are ýтром ("in the morning"), днём ("in the daytime"), веснóй ("in the
spring") and рядом ("side by side"). In some instances, this instrumental
form is all that remains in the language of an obsolete noun: пешкóм ("on
foot").

4. Some adverbial expressions consist of the preposition по and the dative
case of certain adjectives. Examples are: по-прéжнему ("as before"), по-
рáзному ("in various ways"), по-мóему ("in my opinion").

Similar to this group are the expressions with по-plus-adverb meaning
"in (a given language)": по-рýсски ("in Russian"), по-англúйски ("in
English"), по-францýзски ("in French"), по-немéцки ("in German"),
etc.

5. Many adverbs (historically originating as prepositions-plus-nouns) occur
in sense groups based on the following notions: lack of motion, motion
toward, motion away from. Some of these groups are:

(a) вдалú ("in the distance"); вдаль ("into the distance"); úздали
("from afar")
(b) впередú ("at a place ahead"); вперёд ("to the front, forward");
спéреди ("from up ahead, in the front")
(c) позадú ("at the back"); назáд ("to the back"); сзáди ("from the
back")
(d) внизý ("at a place below"); вниз ("downward"); снúзу ("from
below")

PRONOUNS

Many of the words discussed in this chapter have adjectival forms and strictly speaking are pronominal adjectives, but it is convenient and instructive to group them with the pure pronouns to which they are related.

PERSONAL PRONOUNS

The Russian personal pronouns are я ("I, me"), ты ("you"; this is the singular form, used when speaking to one person, and then only to a close friend or relative, small child or animal), он ("he, him, it"), она ("she, her, it"), оно ("it"), мы ("we, us"), вы ("you"; this is not only the plural form, used when speaking to more than one person, but also the polite form of address to a single individual), and они ("they, them"). Like nouns, pronouns are declined; the cases of pronouns have the same uses as for nouns.

SINGULAR

	1ST PERSON	2ND PERSON	3RD PERSON		
			MASC.	FEM.	NEUT.
NOM.	я	ты	он	она	оно
ACC.	меня	тебя	(н)его	(н)её	(н)его
GEN.	меня	тебя	(н)его	(н)её	(н)его
DAT.	мне	тебе	(н)ему	(н)ей	(н)ему
INSTR.	мной	тобой	(н)им	(н)ей	(н)им
PREP.	мне	тебе	нём	ней	нём

PLURAL

	1ST PERSON	2ND PERSON	3RD PERSON
NOM.	мы	вы	они
ACC.	нас	вас	(н)их
GEN.	нас	вас	(н)их

33

DAT.	нам	вам	(н)им
INSTR.	нáми	вáми	(н)úми
PREP.	нас	вас	них

1. When вы refers to one person, long-form adjectives modifying it are in the singular, but short-form adjectives are in the plural:

Вы óчень **сóнный** сегóдня.	You are very *sleepy* today.
Вы **правы́.**	You are *right*.

2. The third person singular forms он, онá and онó refer back to masculine, feminine and neuter nouns, respectively. Thus, он and онá can both mean "it" as well as "he" and "she," respectively:

Я купúл нóвый костю́м. **Он** сéрый.
I bought a new suit. *It* is gray.

Я купúл нóвую шля́пу. **Онá** сéрая.
I bought a new hat. *It* is gray.

3. When the third person pronouns are governed by a preposition, the letter н- is added to the beginning: с ним ("with him"), одúн из них ("one of them").

4. To express "— and I," Russian uses the form мы с —. Thus: мы с брáтом ("my brother and I").

POSSESSIVE PRONOUNS AND ADJECTIVES

The possessive pronouns/adjectives ("my, mine," "your, yours," etc.) that correspond to я, ты, мы and вы are: мой ("my, mine"), твой ("your, yours," familiar singular), наш ("our, ours") and ваш ("your, yours," plural or polite singular). Твой is declined like мой, and ваш like наш:

	SINGULAR			PLURAL
	MASC.	FEM.	NEUT.	ALL GENDERS
NOM.	мой	моя́	моё	мои́
ACC.	мой	мою́	моё	мои́
(ANIM.)	моегó			мои́х
GEN.	моегó	моéй	моегó	мои́х
DAT.	моемý	моéй	моемý	мои́м
INSTR.	мои́м	моéй	мои́м	мои́ми
PREP.	моём	моéй	моём	мои́х

| | SINGULAR | | | PLURAL |
	MASC.	FEM.	NEUT.	ALL GENDERS
NOM.	наш	наша	наше	наши
ACC.	наш	нашу	наше	наши
(ANIM.)	нашего			наших
GEN.	нашего	нашей	нашего	наших
DAT.	нашему	нашей	нашему	нашим
INSTR.	нашим	нашей	нашим	нашими
PREP.	нашем	нашей	нашем	наших

1. Possessive adjectives must agree in gender, number and case with the noun they modify (the thing possessed). Thus, for example, "my sister" will be моя сестра whether the speaker ("I") is masculine or feminine.

2. Note, however, that the possessives that correspond to the third person personal pronouns (singular and plural) are unchanging in form. Corresponding to both он and оно is его ("his", "its"); corresponding to она is её ("her, hers, its"); and corresponding to они is их ("their", "theirs"). These forms never have a prefixed н- when governed by prepositions. The possessive adjective свой ("one's own") is discussed on page 39.

Мы говорим о Москве и **её** зданиях.
We are talking about Moscow and *its* buildings.

3. In Russian, possessives are often omitted where used in English:

Он пишет **матери.**   He is writing *to (his) mother.*

Nor are possessives used with parts of the body, as in the English "My head hurts." Instead, the construction used is: У меня болит голова (LIT.: "By me hurts the head"), or: У него руки замёрзли ("His hands are cold"; LIT.: "By him the hands froze").

In general, the most common way of expressing possession in Russian is by using the preposition у plus the genitive of the noun or pronoun:

У Ивана новая шляпа.   *Ivan has* a new hat.

In the above expression, "new hat," which is the direct object in the English construction, is the subject (nominative) in the Russian.

But when the sentence contains some directed action, the possessor of the object that is undergoing the action must be expressed by a noun or pronoun in the dative case:

Он пожал **мне** руку.
He shook my hand. [LIT.: He shook *to me* the hand.]

Парикма́хер постри́г **ма́льчику** во́лосы.
The barber cut the boy's hair. [LIT.: The barber cut *to the boy* the hair.]

DEMONSTRATIVE PRONOUNS AND ADJECTIVES

The demonstrative adjectives э́тот ("this," PL. "these") and тот ("that," PL. "those") are declined as follows:

		SINGULAR		PLURAL
	MASC.	FEM.	NEUT.	ALL GENDERS
NOM.	э́тот	э́та	э́то	э́ти
ACC.	э́тот	э́ту	э́то	э́ти
(ANIM.)	э́того			э́тих
GEN.	э́того	э́той	э́того	э́тих
DAT.	э́тому	э́той	э́тому	э́тим
INSTR.	э́тим	э́той	э́тим	э́тими
PREP.	э́том	э́той	э́том	э́тих

		SINGULAR		PLURAL
	MASC.	FEM.	NEUT.	ALL GENDERS
NOM.	тот	та	то	те
ACC.	тот	ту	то	те
(ANIM.)	того́			тех
GEN.	того́	той	того́	тех
DAT.	тому́	той	тому́	тем
INSTR.	тем	той	тем	те́ми
PREP.	том	той	том	тех

1. The neuter singular forms — э́то, э́того, etc., and то, того́, etc. — are used as the demonstrative pronouns "this" and "that," respectively. As the introductory word in Russian sentences, э́то can refer to people as well as to things: э́то моя́ жена́ ("this is my wife"). Э́то is sometimes the equivalent of English "it" when the "it" refers not to a specific object (in which case он, она́ or оно́ is needed) but to a fact or state of affairs:

— Говоря́т, что за́втра бу́дет дождь. — Об **э́том** я ничего́ не слы́шал.
"They say that tomorrow there will be rain." "I didn't hear anything about *it*."

Не тот has the meaning of "the wrong —":

| Вы взя́ли **не ту** кни́гу. | You took *the wrong* book. |

2. The demonstrative pronominal adjective тако́й ("such") is declined regularly: така́я де́вушка ("a girl such as this"), така́я краси́вая де́вушка ("such a beautiful girl").

INTERROGATIVE AND RELATIVE PRONOUNS AND ADJECTIVES

1. The interrogative pronoun кто ("who?") is always masculine singular, grammatically; что ("what?") is neuter singular. They are declined as follows:

NOM.	кто	что
ACC.	кого́	что
GEN.	кого́	чего́
DAT.	кому́	чему́
INSTR.	кем	чем
PREP.	ком	чём

Examples of the use of кто and что:

| **Кого́** вы ви́дели? | *Whom* did you see? |
| **Чем** вы пи́шете? | *With what* are you writing? |

2. Кто has an adjectival possessive чей ("whose?"), declined as follows:

		SINGULAR		PLURAL
	MASC.	FEM.	NEUT.	ALL GENDERS
NOM.	чей	чья	чьё	чьи
ACC.	чей	чью	чьё	чьи
(ANIM.)	чьего́			чьих
GEN.	чьего́	чьей	чьего́	чьих
DAT.	чьему́	чьей	чьему́	чьим
INSTR.	чьим	чьей	чьим	чьи́ми
PREP.	чьём	чьей	чьём	чьих

Remember that possessive adjectives must agree in gender, number and case with the thing possessed:

| **Чья** э́та кни́га? | *Whose* book is this? |
| О **чьей** тёте вы говори́те? | About *whose* aunt are you talking? |

3. Two other interrogative pronominal adjectives, both declined like regular hard adjectives, are какóй ("what kind of?") and котóрый ("which?"). Котóрый is now limited in use mainly to the expression котóрый час? ("what time is it?").

4. A number of interrogative pronouns also function as relative pronouns: кто ("who"), что ("what"), какóй ("what"), чей ("whose") and котóрый ("who," "which," "that"). Котóрый, which is used very frequently as a relative, is declined regularly, following the pattern of hard adjectives. Its nominative forms are: MASC. котóрый, FEM. котóрая, NEUT. котóрое, PL. котóрые. It must agree in gender and number with the noun (animate or inanimate) to which it refers, but its case is determined by its function in the relative clause:

Вот кни́га, **котóрую** я чита́л.
Here is the book *that* I was reading.

Вот де́вушка, **котóрой** я дал кни́гу.
There is the girl *to whom* I gave the book.

Кто is used as a relative pronoun in reference to a number of pronouns including тот (тот, кто..., "the one who..."), те (те, кто..., "those who..."), никтó (никтó, кто..., "no one who...") and все (все, кто..., "everyone who...").

Что is not used as frequently as котóрый when the relative refers back to a noun (instead of a pronoun). It is used for the most part with the pronouns всё ("everything") and то (то, что, "that which"):

Вы зна́ете всё, **что** я зна́ю.   You know everything *that* I know.

INDEFINITE AND NEGATIVE PRONOUNS

1. Russian interrogative words in general (and not only pronouns) can be turned into indefinites by adding the unchangeable suffix -то or -нибудь. Thus, ктó-то and ктó-нибудь mean "someone, somebody" or "anyone, anybody"; чтó-то and чтó-нибудь mean "something" or "anything." The кто- and the что- elements are still fully declinable. Ктó-то (like all indefinites with -то) denotes a clear-cut person whose identity is unknown. Ктó-нибудь denotes "anyone at all, anyone in the world":

— Приходи́л ли **ктó-нибудь**? — **Ктó-то** приходи́л, я не зна́ю кто.
"Did *anyone* come by?" "*Somebody* came, (but) I don't know who."

Да́йте биле́т **комý-нибудь** на ýлице.
Give the ticket *to someone* on the street.

2. The negative pronouns никто́ ("no one, nobody") and ничто́ ("nothing") are declined as follows:

NOM.	никто́	ничто́ OR ничего́
ACC.	никого́	ничего́
GEN.	никого́	ничего́
DAT.	никому́	ничему́
INSTR.	нике́м	ниче́м
PREP.	ни о ком	ни о чём

The prepositional is given here with the sample preposition o to show that prepositions are placed between the ни and the кто or что element. This is true for other declensional cases as well:

Ни у **кого́** нет де́нег.   *Nobody* has any money.

REFLEXIVE, EMPHATIC, RECIPROCAL AND OTHER PRONOUNS

1. The reflexive pronoun себя́ ("himself, herself," etc.) never appears as the subject (nominative) of a sentence or clause; it always refers back to that subject, regardless of gender, person or number:

Она́ счита́ет **себя́** о́чень у́мной.
She considers *herself* very intelligent.

Мы счита́ем **себя́** о́чень у́мными.
We consider *ourselves* very intelligent.

Себя́ is declined like the second person pronoun ты: ACC. себя́, GEN. себя́, DAT. себе́, INSTR. собо́й, PREP. себе́. Compare the sentences:

Вади́м говори́т о **себе́**.   Vadim is speaking about *himself*.

Вади́м говори́т о **нём**.
Vadim is speaking about *him* (someone else).

2. The possessive adjective corresponding to себя́ is свой ("one's own"), which is declined like мой. Compare the sentences:

Ива́н написа́л письмо́ **свое́й** сестре́.
Ivan wrote a letter to *his* (*own*) sister.

Ива́н написа́л письмо́ **его́** сестре́.
Ivan wrote a letter to *his* (someone else's) sister.

When the subject is in the first or second person ("I," "we," "you"), there is a choice between свой and the possessives мой, твой, наш or ваш:

Я о́чень люблю́ **мою́** (OR: **свою́**) соба́ку.
I love *my* dog very much.

3. Сам is an emphatic pronominal adjective corresponding to the "myself," "yourself," "himself," etc., in such English phrases as "I myself," "you yourself," "he himself," etc. Сам is declined as follows:

	SINGULAR			PLURAL
	MASC.	FEM.	NEUT.	ALL GENDERS
NOM.	сам	сама́	само́	са́ми
ACC.	самого́	саму́	само́	сами́х
GEN.	самого́	само́й	самого́	сами́х
DAT.	самому́	само́й	самому́	сами́м
INSTR.	сами́м	само́й	сами́м	сами́ми
PREP.	само́м	само́й	само́м	сами́х

When modifying a noun, сам generally precedes it; when modifying a pronoun, it comes after it:

Я ви́дел **саму́** короле́ву в саду́.
I saw the Queen *herself* in the garden.

Она́ **сама́** сши́ла мне э́ту руба́шку.
She *herself* sewed me this shirt.

4. The regularly declined adjective са́мый, which we have already seen used in the superlative degree of adjectives, means "itself," "the very" or "right" when used on its own — with inanimates only:

Мы дое́хали до **са́мого** конца́ ли́нии.
We rode to *the very* end of the line.

Она́ была́ в **са́мом** бою́.
She was *right* in the battle (OR: ... in *the thick of* the battle).

5. The reciprocal pronoun "each other, one another" is expressed in Russian by друг дру́га, in which the first element remains undeclined while the second (declined like a masculine singular noun) conforms to the necessary case requirements:

Они́ ча́сто даю́т **друг дру́гу** пода́рки.
They often give presents *to each other*.

Мы иногда ду́маем **друг о дру́ге**.
We sometimes think *of each other.*

6. The adjective/pronoun весь ("all, entire, whole") is declined as follows:

	SINGULAR			PLURAL
	MASC.	FEM.	NEUT.	ALL GENDERS
NOM.	весь	вся	всё	все
ACC.	весь	всю	всё	все
(ANIM.)	всего́			всех
GEN.	всего́	всей	всего́	всех
DAT.	всему́	всей	всему́	всем
INSTR.	всем	всей	всем	все́ми
PREP.	всём	всей	всём	всех

Examples of the use of весь:

Городо́к **весь** в снегу́.
The town is *all* covered with snow.

Во **всём** ми́ре тако́го живо́тного нет.
There's no such animal in the *whole* world.

The plural (все, всех, etc.) is used pronominally to mean "everyone, everybody"; the neuter singular (всё, всего́, etc.) is used to mean "everything":

Она́ **всех** зна́ет.	She knows *everyone.*
Они́ **всё** зна́ют.	They know *everything.*

PREPOSITIONS

Russian is exceedingly rich in prepositions. Only the most common ones can be considered here, but the basic concepts underlying the use of prepositions will be covered. Each preposition governs at least one grammatical case; that is, the noun or pronoun following it (its object) must have the appropriate case ending. When learning any new preposition not listed here, be sure to learn which case(s) it governs. Those prepositions that are followed by more than one case have correspondingly different shades of meaning; such prepositions will be discussed after those more closely bound to a single case. The special uses of certain prepositions in telling time are given later in the chapter Telling Time (see page 85).

PREPOSITIONS USED WITH THE ACCUSATIVE ONLY

Relatively few prepositions are used with the accusative case only. Among them are:

про ("about, concerning")

моря́к расска́зал де́тям **про** свои́ приключе́ния ("the sailor told the children *about* his adventures"); она́ говори́т **про** э́ту кни́гу ("she is speaking *about* this book")

сквозь ("through")

сквозь тума́н ("*through* the fog"); **сквозь** дыру́ ("*through* a hole")

че́рез ("over, across, through, by way of; in, within; every other")

че́рез мост ("*over* the bridge"); **че́рез** сте́ну ("*through* the wall"); он узна́л о награ́де **че́рез** бра́та ("he learned of the award *through* his brother"); мы пое́хали в Ки́ев **че́рез** Москву́ ("we went to Kiev *by way of* Moscow"); я верну́сь **че́рез** неде́лю ("I'll return *in* a week"); они́ ссо́рились **че́рез** пять мину́т по́сле его́ возвраще́ния ("they quarreled *within* five minutes after his return"); **че́рез** день ("*every other* day")

PREPOSITIONS USED WITH THE GENITIVE ONLY

Prepositions always followed by the genitive, and no other case, include:

без ("without")

без билéта ("*without* a ticket"); **без** исключéния ("*without* exception"); **без** интерéса ("*without* interest")

вмéсто ("instead of")

вмéсто пиджакá ("*instead of* a jacket"); **вмéсто** нас ("*instead of* us")

вокрýг ("round, around, surrounding")

вокрýг дворá ("*around* the yard"); **вокрýг** свéта ("*round* the world")

для ("for, for the sake of")

э́тот я́щик **для** пи́сем ("this drawer is *for* letters"); я сдéлал э́то **для** вас ("I did this *for* your *sake*"); **для** разнообрáзия ("*for* a change")

до ("up to [but not including], as far as, until, before")

до сáмых стен крéпости ("*up to* the very walls of the fortress"); я бýду ждать **до** утрá ("I'll wait *until* morning"); **до** войны́ ("*before* the war")

из ("out of, from out of, made of")

он вы́шел **из** кóмнаты ("he went *out of* the room"); **из** любви́ к рóдине ("*out of* love for one's homeland"); стол **из** дéрева ("the table is *made of* wood"); оди́н **из** студéнтов ("one *of* the students")

из-за ("from behind, from beyond; because of, through")

из-за кустóв ("*from behind* the bushes"); **из-за** грани́цы ("*from* abroad" [LIT.: "*from beyond* the border"]); **из-за** дождя́ ("*because of* the rain"); **из-за** неосторóжности ("*through* carelessness")

крóме ("besides, in addition to, except")

никтó **крóме** вас ("no one *besides* you")

óколо ("near, approximately")

óколо теáтра ("*near* the theater"); **óколо** пяти́ человéк ("*around* five people")

от ("from, away from")

он отошёл **от** стены́ ("he moved *away from* the wall"); **от** Москвы́ до Ки́ева ("*from* Moscow to Kiev"); он получи́л письмо́ **от** сестры́ ("he received a letter *from* his sister"); **от** нача́ла до конца́ ("*from* beginning to end"); он покрасне́л **от** смуще́ния ("he blushed *from* embarrassment")

по́сле ("after, since")

по́сле рабо́ты ("*after* work"); **по́сле** Рождества́ ("*after* Christmas"); **по́сле** его́ возвраще́ния ("*since* his return")

у ("next to, beside, by; at the home of; in the possession of")

у вхо́да ("*by* the entrance"); я был **у** бра́та ("I was *at* my brother*'s*"); **у** моего́ бра́та большо́й дом ("*my brother has* a big house"); **у** меня́ боли́т зуб ("I have a toothache" [LIT.: "*by me* aches a tooth"])

PREPOSITIONS USED WITH THE DATIVE ONLY

Of the prepositions that govern the dative case only, the most important by far is к.

к (**ко** before certain double consonants; "to, toward")

иди́те **к** доске́ ("go *to* the blackboard"); приходи́те **к** нам ("come *to see* us; visit us"); письмо́ **к** сестре́ ("a letter *to* one's sister"); она́ добра́ **ко** мне ("she's kind *to* me")

Two other prepositions governing the dative are благодаря́ ("thanks to, owing to"): **благодаря́** вам ("*thanks to* you"); and согла́сно ("according to"): **согла́сно** Толсто́му ("*according to* Tolstoy").

PREPOSITIONS USED WITH THE INSTRUMENTAL ONLY

Important prepositions used only with the instrumental case are:

ме́жду* ("among, between")

ме́жду дере́вьями ("*among* the trees"); **ме́жду** на́ми ("*between* you and me"); **ме́жду** обе́дом и у́жином ("*between* lunch and dinner"); **ме́жду** окно́м и две́рью ("*between* the window and the door")

---

* Ме́жду occasionally occurs with the accusative; the meaning is the same.

над (**на́до** before certain double consonants; "over, above," whether motion is involved or not)

над на́ми лета́л самолёт ("a plane flew *over* us"); **над** у́ровнем мо́ря ("*above* sea level"); он подня́лся **на́до** мной по ле́стнице ("he climbed *to a place above* me on the ladder")

пе́ред (**пе́редо** before certain double consonants; "before, in front of, prior to")

пе́ред две́рью ("*in front of* the door"); **пе́ред** мои́м отъе́здом ("*just before* my departure"); **пе́ред** обе́дом ("before dinner")

PREPOSITIONS USED WITH THE PREPOSITIONAL ONLY

The only important preposition used exclusively with the prepositional case is при.

при ("at the time of, in the presence of, with")

при Ста́лине ("*during the* Stalin *era*"); не говори́те так **при** мое́й ма́тери! ("don't talk that way *in front of* my mother!"); **при** уча́стии дете́й ("*with* the children's participation")

PREPOSITIONS USED WITH MORE THAN ONE CASE

в (**во** before certain double consonants; WITH ACCUSATIVE: "to, into; per"; WITH PREPOSITIONAL: "in, at")

ACC.: вчера́ мы пришли́ **в** Москву́ ("we came *to* Moscow yesterday"); он вошёл **в** ку́хню ("he went *into* the kitchen"); три ра́за **в** неде́лю ("three times *per* week")

PREP.: роди́ться **в** Москве́ ("to be born *in* Moscow"); **в** ку́хне ("*in* the kitchen"); **в** конто́ре ("*at* the office"); **в** гора́х ("*in* the mountains"); **в** ста́рости ("*in* one's old age"); **в** отча́янии ("*in* despair")

за (WITH NOMINATIVE, together with что: "what sort of?"; WITH ACCUSATIVE: "[to a place] behind or beyond; for, in return for; in place of; in"; WITH INSTRUMENTAL: "[at a place] behind or beyond; at; for; after")

NOM.: **что** э́то **за** безобра́зие? ("*what sort of* mess is this?"); **что** э́то **за** пти́ца? ("*what kind of* bird is this?")

ACC.: они́ пое́хали **за** грани́цу ("they went abroad" [LIT.: "they went *beyond* the border"]); со́лнце зашло́ **за** горизо́нт ("the sun went *below* the horizon"); маши́на заверну́ла **за** у́гол ("the car went *around* the corner"); они́ се́ли **за** стол ("they sat down *at* the table"); спаси́бо **за** ва́шу по́мощь ("thanks *for* your help"); я бу́ду рабо́тать **за** бра́та ("I'll work *in place of* my brother"); мы все **за** мир ("we are all *for* peace"); я прочита́л кни́гу **за** одну́ неде́лю ("I finished reading the book *in* one week")

INSTR.: сейча́с он **за** грани́цей ("he is now abroad"); со́лнце уже́ **за** горизо́нтом ("the sun is already *below* the horizon"); парикма́хер-ская **за** угло́м ("the barbershop is *just around* the corner"); у него́ есть да́ча **за** го́родом ("he has a summer house *outside of* town"); они́ сиде́ли **за** столо́м ("they were sitting *at* the table"); **за** за́втраком ("at breakfast"); я зайду́ **за** ва́ми в по́лдень ("I'll come *for* you at noon"); день **за** днём ("day *after* day")

на (WITH ACCUSATIVE: "on[to]; to [instead of в with certain nouns]; by; for"; WITH PREPOSITIONAL: "on, at")

ACC.: он пове́сил карти́ну **на** сте́ну ("he hung the picture *on* the wall"); **на** заво́д, ста́нцию, рабо́ту, собра́ние ("*to* the factory, the station, work, the meeting"); он ста́рше меня́ **на** пять лет ("he's five years older than I am" [LIT.: "he's older than I *by* five years"]); материа́л **на** пла́тье ("material *for* a dress"); что у нас бу́дет **на** обе́д? ("what will we have *for* dinner?")

PREP.: он **на** рабо́те ("he's *at* work"); карти́на виси́т **на** стене́ ("a picture hangs *on* the wall"); мы прие́хали сюда́ **на** авто́бусе ("we came here *on* the bus [OR: *by* bus]")

о (**об** before vowels, **о́бо** before certain double consonants; WITH ACCUSATIVE: "against [in actions of contact]"; WITH PREPOSITIONAL: "about, concerning")

ACC.: кора́бль разби́лся **о** ска́лы ("the ship broke up *on* the rocks"); опира́ться **о** де́рево ("to lean *against* a tree")

PREP.: он рассказа́л нам **о** своём путеше́ствии ("he told us *about* his trip"); мы говори́м **о** пого́де ("we are talking *about* the weather")

по (WITH ACCUSATIVE: "up to [and including]; apiece, each"; WITH DATIVE: "along, through; according to; on, by, in; apiece,* each")

---

* When meaning "apiece," по is followed by the accusative when two or more items are distributed to each party; by the dative when only one item is distributed to each party.

ACC.: водá поднялáсь емý **по** колéни ("the water rose *to* his knees"); с понедéльника **по** четвéрг ("from Monday *through* Thursday"); мать раздалá дéтям **по** два я́блока ("the mother gave the children two apples *apiece*"); э́ти карандаши́ стóят **по** дéсять копéек ("these pencils cost ten kopecks *each*")

DAT.: **по** дорóге ("*along* the road"); **по** пáрку ("*through* the park"); **по** истóрии Росси́и ("*throughout* the history of Russia"); **по** плáну ("*according to* plan"); **по** телеви́дению ("*on* television"); удáрили егó **по** головé ("he was hit *on* the head"); **по** оши́бке ("*by* mistake"); **по** пóчте ("*by* mail"); **по** егó мнéнию ("*in* his opinion"); специали́ст **по** рýсской литератýре ("*a specialist in* Russian literature"); он рабóтает **по** вечерáм ("he works evenings"); студéнты разъéхались **по** домáм на кани́кулы ("the students went *to* their homes for the vacation"—i.e., they dispersed, *each* going to his own home); мать раздалá дéтям **по** однóмý я́блоку ("the mother gave the children one apple *apiece*")

под (**пóдо** before certain double consonants; WITH ACCUSATIVE: "[to a place] under, below"; WITH INSTRUMENTAL: "[at a place] under, below")

ACC.: постáвьте портфéль **под** стол ("put your briefcase *under* the table")

INSTR.: мáльчик спал **под** дéревом ("a boy was sleeping *under* a tree"); **под** горóй ("*at the bottom of* the hill"); **под** руковóдством Лéнина ("*under* Lenin's leadership")

с (**со** before certain double consonants; WITH ACCUSATIVE: "approximately; the size of"; WITH GENITIVE: "from off the top of [with verbs of action]; from [instead of из with certain nouns]; since"; WITH INSTRUMENTAL: "with, together with, and")

ACC.: мы прóжили там **с** мéсяц ("we spent *about* a month there"); он рóстом **с** брáта ("he is *about* the same height as his brother"); грáдины **с** я́блоки ("hailstones *the size of* apples")

GEN.: он взял кни́гу **со** столá ("he took the book *from* [OR: *off*] the table"); **с** завóда, стáнции, рабóты, собрáния ("*from* the factory, the station, work, the meeting"); скóлько с меня́? ("how much do I owe?" [LIT.: "how much *from* me?"]); с рýсского на англи́йский ("*from* Russian into English"); они́ здесь с понедéльника ("they've been here *since* Monday")

INSTR.: онá пошлá в бýлочную **со** мной ("she went to the bakery *with* me"); **с** захóдом сóлнца ("*with* the setting of the sun"); хлеб **с** сы́ром ("bread *and* cheese")

INTERRELATION OF PREPOSITIONS IN SENTENCES OF MOTION

It is clear from the above listing that the notion of location in a place, and of various types of motion to and from a place, have much to do with the proper choice of prepositions and the cases they govern. It is convenient to recapitulate some of the relevant prepositions in a grouping that clarifies their interrelation:

LOCATION (ABSENCE OF MOTION)	MOTION TOWARD	MOTION AWAY FROM
в + prepositional "in, at"	**в** + accusative "into, to"	**из** + genitive "out of, from"
Он **в** теа́тре. He is *in* the theater.	Он пошёл **в** теа́тр. He went *into* the theater.	Он вы́шел **из** теа́тра. He went *out of* the theater.
на + prepositional "on, at"	**на** + accusative "on(to); to"	**с** + genitive "off of; from"
Кни́га **на** столе́. The book is *on* the table.	Он положи́л кни́гу **на** стол. He put the book *on* the table.	Он взял кни́гу **со** стола́. He took the book *off* the table.
Он **на** собра́нии. He is *at* the meeting.	Он пошёл **на** собра́ние. He went *to* the meeting.	Он пришёл **с** собра́ния. He has come *from* the meeting.
у + genitive "next to, beside, by"	**к** + dative "to(ward), up to the side of"	**от** + genitive "away from the side of"
Он **у** окна́. He is *by* the window.	Он подошёл **к** окну́. He went up *to* the window.	Он отошёл **от** окна́. He went away *from* the window.
Я был **у** бра́та. I was *at* my brother's.	Я пошёл **к** бра́ту. I went *to* my brother's.	Я ушёл **от** бра́та. I went away *from* my brother's.

за + instrumental	за + accusative	из-за + genitive
"behind, beyond"	"behind, beyond"	"from behind, from beyond"

Он живёт за границей.	Он поéхал за грани́цу.	Он верну́лся из-за грани́цы.
He lives abroad.	He went abroad.	He returned *from* abroad.

под + instrumental	под + accusative	из-под + genitive
"under, below"	"under, below"	"out from under"

Ребёнок игра́л под столо́м.	Ребёнок запо́лз под стол.	Ребёнок вы́полз из-под стола́.
The baby played *under* the table.	The baby crawled *under* the table.	The baby crawled *out from under* the table.

Над ("over, above") and пéред ("in front of") are always followed by the instrumental, whether motion is involved or not.

CONJUNCTIONS

Like English, Russian contains two general types of conjunction: coordinating and subordinating. Only the most common coordinating and subordinating conjunctions are given here together with examples of their use.

COORDINATING CONJUNCTIONS

и ("and," linking like parts of speech and compatible ideas)

у меня́ я́блоки **и** апельси́ны ("I have apples *and* oranges"); он у́чится чита́ть **и** писа́ть ("he is learning to read *and* write")

и ... и ("both ... and")

и Ива́н, **и** Михаи́л бу́дут рабо́тать за вас ("*both* Ivan *and* Mikhail will work in place of you"); он говори́т **и** по-францу́зски, **и** по-ру́сски ("he speaks *both* French *and* Russian")

ни ... ни ("neither ... nor")

ни Ива́н, **ни** Михаи́л не бу́дет рабо́тать за вас ("*neither* Ivan *nor* Mikhail will work in place of you"); он не говори́т **ни** по-францу́зски, **ни** по-ру́сски ("he speaks *neither* French *nor* Russian")

а ("and, but, whereas," linking contrasting but not antithetical ideas)

его́ пальто́ чёрное, **а** моё се́рое ("his coat is black *and* mine is gray"); она́ хо́чет ждать, **а** я не хочу́ ("she wants to wait *but* I don't")

но ("but," linking incompatible or antithetical ideas)

он был ма́ленький, **но** хра́брый ("he was small, *but* brave"); я вам помогу́, **но** вы должны́ сказа́ть мне пра́вду ("I will help you, *but* you must tell me the truth")

и́ли ("or")

э́то серебро́ **и́ли** зо́лото? ("is that silver *or* gold?")

50

и́ли ... и́ли ("either ... or")

и́ли Ива́н, **и́ли** Михаи́л бу́дет рабо́тать за вас (*"either* Ivan *or* Mikhail will work in place of you")

SUBORDINATING CONJUNCTIONS

что ("that," used after verbs of saying, thinking, believing, etc.)

я зна́ю, **что** вы съе́здили за грани́цу ("I know *that* you went abroad"); я ду́маю, **что** он до́ма ("I think *that* he is at home")

что́бы ("that," often unexpressed in English)

(a) With the past tense after verbs of request, command, warning, fearing or doubting:

я попроси́л, **что́бы** он зашёл ко мне сего́дня ("I asked him to stop by today"); прокуро́р потре́бовал, **что́бы** обвиня́емый призна́лся в преступле́нии ("the prosecutor demanded *that* the accused admit to his crime"); команди́р приказа́л, **что́бы** войска́ отступи́ли ("the commander ordered the troops to retreat"); я боя́лся, **что́бы** он не пришёл ("I was *afraid* that he might come")

(b) As a conjunction of purpose with the meaning "in order to, in order that, so that": (1) with an infinitive if the subject of the dependent clause is the same as the subject of the main clause; and (2) with the past tense if there is a change of subject. (When serving as a conjunction of purpose, что́бы is usually omitted when the main verb is a verb of motion when there is no change of subject.)

они́ пригласи́ли меня́, **что́бы** узна́ть о мое́й но́вой кни́ге ("they invited me *in order to* find out about my new book"); гра́ждане собра́лись, **что́бы** обсужда́ть вопро́с ("the citizens assembled *in order to* discuss the issue"); я встал, **что́бы** он мог сесть ("I stood up *so that* he could sit down"); он пришёл, **что́бы** верну́ть твою́ кни́гу ("he came *in order to* return your book")

потому́ что ("because")

я сча́стлив, **потому́ что** сего́дня мой день рожде́ния ("I am happy *because* today is my birthday")

из-за того́, что ("because," with the implication of failure or trouble)

из-за того́, что вы опозда́ли, мы не успе́ли на по́езд ("*because* you arrived late, we didn't make the train")

так как ("because, since")

> **так как** я знал, что вы ра́но ложи́тесь спать, я не звони́л ("*since* I knew that you go to bed early, I didn't telephone")

хотя́ ("although")

> **хотя́** бы́ло уже́ по́здно, он реши́л пойти́ ("*although* it was already late, he decided to go")

как ("like, as")

> я люблю́ его́ **как** сы́на ("I love him *like* a son")

до того́, как ("before")

> **до того́, как** он уе́хал, он позвони́л мне ("*before* he left he telephoned me")

пе́ред тем, как ("just before")

> **пе́ред тем, как** он уе́хал, он позвони́л мне ("*just before* he left he telephoned me")

по́сле того́, как ("after")

> **по́сле того́, как** он вы́шел из ко́мнаты, она́ распла́калась ("*after* he left the room she burst into tears")

с тех пор, как ("since")

> говоря́т, что он о́чень измени́лся **с тех пор, как** мы разлучи́лись ("they say that he has changed a lot *since* we parted company")

пока́ ... не ("until")

> я ничего́ никому́ не скажу́, **пока́** вы **не** дади́те разреше́ние ("I will not tell anyone anything *until* you give permission")

по ме́ре того́, как ("as, in proportion as")

> **по ме́ре того́, как** милиционе́ры приближа́лись, толпа́ крича́ла ("*as* the police approached the crowd shouted")

VERBS: FORMATION

TENSE AND ASPECT

The Russian verb system has only three tenses: present, past and future. However, Russian has a categorization of verbs that has almost no parallel in English: nearly every Russian verb is of one of two **aspects**, imperfective or perfective. It takes some time and effort to gain a comprehensive understanding of the ways in which these two aspects are used, but the most basic and important distinction between them is readily understandable:

Imperfective verbs describe actions without reference to the completion of those actions. They may describe an action in general ("Fish *swim* but people *walk*"), or an action in progress ("She *was reading* when I called"), or a repeated or habitual action ("They *skate* every day").

Perfective verbs describe actions that have been or will be completed ("She *has read* the book"; "She *will read* the book").

Thus, in Russian, verbs almost always come in pairs, a given verb in English being represented by two verbs in Russian to meet the two aspect requirements. For example, to correspond to the English "to read," Russian has both the imperfective verb читáть (implying "to read in general, to read habitually, to be reading") and the perfective verb прочитáть (implying "to read through, to finish reading"). In this case, it is a prefix (про-) that indicates the difference; sometimes it is a change in the stem (different vowel or inserted syllable); sometimes two completely different verbs are used.

THE INFINITIVE

The form in which Russian verbs are entered into dictionaries is the infinitive, corresponding to the English "to stroll," "to be," etc. Most verbs have infinitives ending in -ть. In general, the infinitive is used in much the same way as in English:

Я люблю **гуля́ть** по пáрку.   I love *to stroll* through the park.

Быть иль не **быть**, вот в чём вопрóс.
To be or not *to be*, that is the question. [From Pasternak's translation of *Hamlet*.]

THE PRESENT TENSE

Imperfective verbs have three separate tenses: present, past and future. Since the present tense by its nature can never describe a completed action, and completed action is the hallmark of the perfective aspect, perfective verbs have only two separate tenses: past and future. The Russian present tense corresponds to all the different English constructions denoting present time: "he reads," "he is reading," "he does read."

In the present tense, the overwhelming majority of Russian verbs have a different ending for each of the personal pronouns. These endings are added to the stem after dropping the -ть of the infinitive (and often the vowel preceding the -ть). There are two chief sets of these personal endings. In Conjugation I, e is the characteristic vowel of the endings, appearing in the forms for ты, он (or она́ or оно́), мы and вы. In Conjugation II, the characteristic vowel in the corresponding endings is и. Our model verb for Conjugation I will be the imperfective verb чита́ть ("to read"); for Conjugation II, the imperfective verb говори́ть ("to speak"):

CONJUGATION I

	SINGULAR		PLURAL	
1ST PERS.	я чита́ю	I read	мы чита́ем	we read
2ND PERS.	ты чита́ешь	you read	вы чита́ете	you read
3RD PERS.	он чита́ет	he reads	они́ чита́ют	they read

CONJUGATION II

	SINGULAR		PLURAL	
1ST PERS.	я говорю́	I speak	мы говори́м	we speak
2ND PERS.	ты говори́шь	you speak	вы говори́те	you speak
3RD PERS.	он говори́т	he speaks	они́ говоря́т	they speak

1. When the verb stem ends in ж-, ц-, ч-, ш- or щ-, the -ю ending of the first person singular becomes -у and the -ят ending of the third person plural becomes -ат. Thus, for the imperfective Conjugation II verb точи́ть ("to sharpen"), the first person singular is точу́ and the third person plural is то́чат.

2. Remember that the third person singular is the form to use with any of the third person singular personal pronouns (он, она́ or оно́).

3. Every Russian verb in the present tense will conform to one of three possible stress patterns: (1) the stress will be on the stem throughout (as for чита́ть); (2) the stress will be on the endings throughout (as for говори́ть); or (3) there will be shifting stress. In the shifting stress pattern, the stress falls on the ending of the first person singular, then shifts to the stem for all other persons. Thus, the present tense of точи́ть is: точу́, то́чишь, то́чит, то́чим, то́чите, то́чат.

When the stress falls on the endings throughout in Conjugation I, those endings then become: -у́, -ёшь, -ёт, -ём, -ёте, -у́т. Thus, the imperfective verb нести́ ("to carry") has the present tense: несу́, несёшь, несёт, несём, несёте, несу́т.

4. We have already seen consonant mutation at work in the comparative degree of adjectives: ти́хий ("quiet")/ти́ше ("quieter"). It may also take place in the present tense of verbs; when it occurs, it does so in a systematic and predictable way. In Conjugation I it affects every form; in Conjugation II, only the first person singular. Thus, the imperfective Conjugation I verb писа́ть ("to write") drops the a as well as the ть of the infinitive before adding the personal endings; the c at the end of the stem mutates into ш; and we get the present tense: пишу́, пи́шешь, пи́шет, пи́шем, пи́шете, пи́шут. The imperfective Conjugation II verb сиде́ть ("to sit") has the stem сид- and the д mutates to ж in the first person singular, giving: сижу́, сиди́шь, сиди́т, сиди́м, сиди́те, сидя́т. Among the most common patterns of mutation of consonants or consonant clusters at the end of verb stems are: (1) г, д and з may mutate to ж; (2) с, к, т and ц may mutate to ч; (3) х may mutate to ш; and (4) ск and ст may mutate to щ. Additional examples: указа́ть ("to show")/укажу́, ука́жешь, etc.; пла́кать ("to cry, weep")/пла́чу, пла́чешь, etc.; иска́ть ("to look for, seek")/ищу́, и́щешь, etc.; грусти́ть ("to grieve, mourn")/грущу́, грусти́шь, etc.

It will be noted that, by keeping in mind the rules about the distribution of stress and of mutated consonants within the present tense, you can conjugate any verb in that tense if you know the first and second person singular forms in addition to the infinitive. For instance, from писа́ть/ пишу́, пи́шешь one learns that the stem ends with the c, which is mutated into ш; that the verb belongs to Conjugation I (because the vowel of the ending is e and because the mutation extends beyond the first person singular; and that the stress is a shifting one. From this point on, there will be no need to give the full present conjugation of verbs (unless they have further irregularities), but merely give these three forms.

5. In verbs with stems ending in б-, в-, м-, п- or ф-, the letter л is inserted between the stem and the present tense endings (in all forms, for Conjugation I; in the first person singular, for Conjugation II). All such verbs have shifting stress. Examples: люби́ть ("to love, like")/люблю́, лю́бишь; лови́ть ("to catch")/ловлю́, ло́вишь; дрема́ть ("to doze")/дремлю́, дре́млешь; утопи́ть ("to drown")/утоплю́, уто́пишь.

PATTERNS OF PRESENT TENSE CONJUGATION

In the following arrangement of Russian verbs by their present tense, each group is represented by one or more typical verbs shown in the infinitive and in the first and second persons singular (more forms given where necessary). Remember that rules of consonant mutation and stress may account for specific differences within each group. Mutation can only come into play where a mutable consonant immediately precedes the personal endings.

Infinitives Ending in -атъ

All verbs with infinitives ending in -атъ are Conjugation I except for those in group 7.

1. Читáть ("to read")/читáю, читáешь is one of thousands of verbs in which the stem is the infinitive minus the -ть.

2. Писáть ("to write")/пишý, пúшешь is one of about 60 verbs in which -атъ is dropped to find the stem, and there is a mutation wherever possible. All verbs formed on the root -казáть (basic meaning: "to show, to tell") are in this group, as well as such common verbs as двúгать ("to move"), искáть ("to seek"), плáкать ("to cry"), прáтать ("to hide") and рéзать ("to cut").

3. Another group of verbs that drop -атъ begin with consonant clusters; e.g.: ждать ("to wait")/жду, ждёшь; врать ("to tell lies")/вру, врёшь. In some cases a vowel is inserted between the stem consonants, and there is stress on the personal endings; e.g.: брать ("to take")/ берý, берёшь; звать ("to call")/зовý, зовёшь.

4. Трéбовать ("to demand")/трéбую, трéбуешь is one of thousands of verbs in which the stem is formed by dropping the -овать and inserting y before the personal endings. Many loan words from other languages are formed in this way; e.g.: ликвидúровать ("to liquidate")/ликвидúрую, ликвидúруешь. When the infinitive ending is -евать, the inserted vowel is ю, as in воевáть ("to wage war")/воюю, воюешь, unless this is precluded by the nature of the preceding consonant, such as the ч in ночевáть ("to spend the night")/ночýю, ночýешь.

5. A small category consists of verbs built on the roots -давáть (basic meaning: "to give"), -знавáть (basic meaning: "to know") and -ставáть (basic meaning: "to stand, to stay"). The pattern in this group is to drop the -вать before adding the personal endings: давáть ("to give")/даю, даёшь.

6. Some verbs have н inserted before the personal endings. Sometimes the a of the infinitive ending is retained: встать ("to get up")/встáну, встáнешь. Sometimes it is not: начáть ("to begin")/начнý, начнёшь.

7. Only about 30 verbs ending in -ать are Conjugation II. In these verbs, for which the -ать is dropped, the stem usually ends in ж-, ч-, ш- or щ-. Examples: дрожáть ("to tremble")/дрожý, дрожúшь; держáть ("to hold")/держý, дéржишь. The verb бежáть ("to run") has the irregular conjugation бегý, бежúшь, бежúт, бежúм, бежúте, бегýт. The verb спать ("to sleep") is conjugated сплю, спишь, etc. The verb гнать ("to drive animals") and the verbs derived from it by means of prefixes, such as догнáть ("to catch up with"), have an inserted о: гоню́, гóнишь.

Infinitives Ending in -ять

Infinitives ending in -ять are all Conjugation I except for боя́ться ("to fear") and стоя́ть ("to stand").

1. For most of these verbs, the -ять is dropped, leaving a stem that ends in a vowel; e.g.: се́ять ("to sow")/се́ю, се́ешь.

2. When the -ять is preceded by н, the -ять is dropped and им is inserted before the personal endings: снять ("to take off")/сниму́, сни́мешь; обня́ть ("to embrace")/обниму́, обни́мешь. Somewhat irregular verbs in this group are приня́ть ("to take, to accept")/приму́, при́мешь; поня́ть ("to understand")/пойму́, поймёшь; and заня́ть ("to borrow")/займу́, займёшь.

Infinitives Ending in -ить

1. Говори́ть ("to speak")/говорю́, говори́шь is one of thousands of verbs in which the stem is the infinitive minus the -ить and the first person singular mutates where possible.

2. A small subgroup has an inserted ь and Conjugation I endings; e.g.: бить ("to beat")/бью, бьёшь, бьёт, бьём, бьёте, бьют. Other important verbs in this group are пить ("to drink"), лить ("to pour"), шить ("to sew") and вить ("to wind").

3. The verb жить ("to live") conjugates живý, живёшь, живёт, живём, живéте, живýт. The verb брить ("to shave") conjugates бре́ю, бре́ешь, etc.

Infinitives Ending in -еть

1. In one group, of Conjugation I, only the -ть is dropped: уме́ть ("to be able, to know how")/уме́ю, уме́ешь.

2. In another group, of Conjugation II, the -еть is dropped, leaving a stem that ends in a consonant; e.g.: ви́деть ("to see")/ви́жу, ви́дишь; лете́ть ("to fly")/лечу́, лети́шь.

3. When the full infinitive ending is -ере́ть, that whole ending is dropped and р is inserted before the stressed Conjugation I personal endings: умере́ть ("to die")/умру́, умрёшь. When a prefix causes an uncomfortable consonant cluster, о is inserted after it: стере́ть ("to wipe, to clean")/сотру́, сотрёшь; отпере́ть ("to unlock")/отопру́, отопрёшь.

4. The verb петь ("to sing") conjugates пою́, поёшь, поёт, поём, поёте, пою́т. The verb оде́ть ("to clothe") conjugates оде́ну, оде́нешь, etc.

Infinitives Ending in -оть

Verbs with infinitives ending in -оть are Conjugation I. The -оть is dropped; e.g.: боро́ться* ("to fight")/борю́сь, бо́решься. The verb моло́ть ("to grind") has a change in its stem vowel: мелю́, ме́лешь.

Infinitives Ending in -ыть

Verbs with infinitives ending in -ыть are Conjugation I. The -ыть is dropped and a stressed о is inserted before the personal endings: мыть ("to wash")/мо́ю, мо́ешь; откры́ть ("to open")/откро́ю, откро́ешь. The verb плыть ("to swim") conjugates плыву́, плывёшь, etc.

Infinitives Ending in -уть

Verbs with infinitives ending in -уть are Conjugation I. The -ть is dropped: дуть ("to blow")/ду́ю, ду́ешь. When the -уть is preceded by н (-нуть verbs are almost always perfectives), the -уть is dropped and the first person singular ends in -у even when unstressed: исче́знуть ("to disappear")/исче́зну, исче́знешь.

---

* The significance of the verbal suffixes -ся and -сь is explained on page 64.

Infinitives Ending in Other Than Vowel-Plus-ть

1. идти́ ("to walk, to go on foot") is conjugated иду́, идёшь, etc. Прийти́ ("to arrive, to come on foot") conjugates приду́, придёшь. Пойти́ ("to go") gives пойду́, пойдёшь.

2. In verbs with infinitives ending in -сти or -сть (they are Conjugation I, with stressed endings), the с is the end of the stem and usually mutates into д or т (sometimes б) before the personal endings are added; e.g.: вести́ ("to lead")/веду́, ведёшь; плести́ ("to weave")/плету́, плетёшь; укра́сть ("to steal")/украду́, украдёшь; грести́ ("to row, to rake")/гребу́, гребёшь. The verb сесть ("to sit down") has a change in its stem vowel: ся́ду, ся́дешь. Two verbs in which the с is not mutated are нести́ ("to carry")/несу́, несёшь and трясти́ ("to shake")/трясу́, трясёшь.

3. In verbs with infinitives ending in -зти or -зть (Conjugation I, stressed endings), the з is the end of the stem but there is no mutation: везти́ ("to haul")/везу́, везёшь.

4. In verbs with infinitives ending in -чь (Conjugation I), the -чь is dropped and а г or к is inserted that is subject to mutation (into ж and ч, respectively) in the second and third persons singular and the first and second persons plural; e.g.: мочь ("to be able")/могу́, мо́жешь, мо́жет, мо́жем, мо́жете, мо́гут; печь ("to bake")/пеку́, печёшь, печёт, печём, печёте, пеку́т. The verb лечь ("to lie down") has a change in its stem vowel: ля́гу, ля́жешь, etc.

Some Additional Irregular Verbs

Six important additional irregular verbs are: дать ("to give")/дам, дашь, даст, дади́м, дади́те, даду́т; есть ("to eat")/ем, ешь, ест, еди́м, еди́те, едя́т; е́хать ("to go by conveyance")/е́ду, е́дешь, etc.; взять ("to take")/возьму́, возьмёшь, etc.; проче́сть ("to read through")/прочту́, прочтёшь, etc.; хоте́ть ("to want, to like")—which has a Conjugation I singular and a Conjugation II plural—хочу́, хо́чешь, хо́чет, хоти́м, хоти́те, хотя́т.

THE IMPERATIVE OR COMMAND FORM

The imperative form of verbs, used to make commands or requests (e.g., "Come here!" "Read this book!"), is closely connected to the present tense conjugation pattern of the verb.

1. When the second person singular form of the present tense has a vowel just before the personal ending -ешь or -ёшь, then the imperative is formed by dropping that ending and adding -й or -йте. (The ending -й gives the familiar singular command form, corresponding to the personal pronoun ты; the ending -йте gives the familiar plural command form, but also the polite form singular or plural, corresponding to the personal pronoun вы. Note, however, that normally no subject pronoun is used with the imperative itself.)

Thus, using the same model verbs as in the preceding section on conjugation patterns, we get:

		IMPERATIVE	
INFINITIVE	2ND PERS. SING.	FAMILIAR SING.	POLITE OR PL.
читáть ("to read")	читáешь	читáй	читáйте
трéбовать ("to demand")	трéбуешь	трéбуй	трéбуйте
сéять ("to sow")	сéешь	сей	сéйте
брить ("to shave")	брéешь	брей	брéйте
петь ("to sing")	поёшь	пой	пóйте
мыть ("to wash")	мóешь	мой	мóйте
дуть ("to blow")	дýешь	дуй	дýйте

2. When the personal endings of the present tense are preceded by a consonant, the choice of imperative endings depends on the stress pattern of that conjugation. (a) When the present tense stress falls on any ending at all (the first person singular is a good indicator for this), drop the personal ending of the third person plural (-ут, -ят or -ют) and add -й (familiar) or -йте (polite). (b) When the present tense stress falls on the stem throughout, drop the third person plural ending and add -ь (familiar) or -ьте (polite). (c) When the personal endings of the present tense are preceded by two consonants, the imperative endings are -и and -ите, regardless of present tense stress.

Referring again to the model verbs in the conjugation section:

			IMPERATIVE	
INFINITIVE	1ST PERS. SING.	3RD PERS. PL.	FAMILIAR SING.	POLITE OR PL.
(a) писáть ("to write")	пишý	пи́шут	пиши́	пиши́те
брать ("to take")	берý	берýт	бери́	бери́те
бежáть ("to run")	бегý	бегýт	беги́	беги́те
гнать ("to drive animals")	гоню́	гóнят	гони́	гони́те
снять ("to take off")	снимý	сни́мут	сними́	сними́те

говори́ть ("to speak")	говорю́	говоря́т	говори́	говори́те
жить ("to live")	живу́	живу́т	живи́	живи́те
лете́ть ("to fly")	лечу́	летя́т	лети́	лети́те
боро́ться ("to fight")	борю́сь	бо́рются	бори́сь	бори́тесь
плыть ("to swim")	плыву́	плыву́т	плыви́	плыви́те
идти́ ("to walk")	иду́	иду́т	иди́	иди́те
вести́ ("to lead")	веду́	веду́т	веди́	веди́те
везти́ ("to haul")	везу́	везу́т	вези́	вези́те
печь ("to bake")	пеку́	пеку́т	пеки́	пеки́те
(b) встать ("to get up")	вста́ну	вста́нут	встань	вста́ньте
оде́ть ("to clothe")	оде́ну	оде́нут	оде́нь	оде́ньте
(c) ждать ("to wait")	жду	ждут	жди	жди́те
спать ("to sleep")	сплю	спят	спи	спи́те
умере́ть ("to die")	умру́	умру́т	умри́	умри́те
исче́знуть ("to disappear")	исче́зну	исче́знут	исче́зни	исче́зните
взять ("to take")	возьму́	возьму́т	возьми́	возьми́те
проче́сть ("to read through")	прочту́	прочту́т	прочти́	прочти́те

3. Still referring to the model verbs of the conjugation section: there are irregularities in the group -дава́ть (-знава́ть, -става́ть), which forms the imperative as -дава́й, -дава́йте, etc.; and in the group бить (пить, лить, etc.), which forms the imperative as бей, бе́йте, etc.

The verb дать ("to give") has the imperative дай, да́йте; the verb есть has the imperative ешь, е́шьте. The imperfective verb быть ("to be"; not in the section on the present tense because its present tense is no longer expressed in modern Russian*) has the imperative будь, бу́дьте.

4. The expression "let's" (as in "let's go!"), sometimes referred to as the first-person imperative, is most often conveyed in Russian by the first person plural form of the present tense (which is then not preceded by the pronoun мы): пойдём ("let's go!"). The suffix -те may be added if more politeness is desired: пойдёмте.

The expression "let him" (or "her," "it" or "them"; as in "let him come!"), sometimes referred to as the third-person imperative, is conveyed by the word пусть (or пуска́й) plus the third person ending (singular or plural as the situation demands) of the present tense: пусть он придёт (or пуска́й оп придёт, "let him come!"); пусть пойду́т, е́сли хотя́т ("let them go if they want").

---

* Есть ("is"), not to be confused with the infinitive есть ("to eat"), is a relic of the present tense of быть; it is often used with the meaning "there is, there are": есть то́лько оди́н спо́соб его́ убеди́ть ("*there is* only one way to persuade him").

THE PAST TENSE

The Russian past tense corresponds to all the English constructions denoting past time: "he wrote," "he did write," "he was writing," "he used to write," "he (would) often write," "he had written," "he had been writing." It is formed the same way for both perfective and imperfective verbs. For most verbs, the -ть is dropped from the infinitive and the ending -л, -ла, -ло or -ли is added.

1. These endings of the past tense, unlike those of the present, do not correspond to *persons* (first, second, third) but to the *gender* and *number* of the verb's subject. Thus—using the verb писáть ("to write")—писáл is the form used whenever the subject is a masculine singular, whether it is "I" (a male speaking), "you" (ты; a male being familiarly addressed), "he" or a masculine singular noun; писáла is the form used whenever the corresponding subjects are female or feminine (я, ты, онá or a feminine singular noun); писáло when they are neuter. The form писáли is used for all plurals, regardless of gender, and for the pronoun вы (whether familiar plural, polite singular or polite plural).

2. The past tense exhibits fewer variations and irregularities than the present, but the following should be noted:

(a) In the verb group with infinitives ending in -ерéть (умерéть, "to die"; терéть, "to rub"; отперéть, "to unlock"; etc.), the -еть is dropped before adding the past endings; the masculine singular has no -л (in monosyllables, the е before the р becomes ё): умерéть/ýмер, умерлá, ýмерло, ýмерли; терéть/тёр, тёрла, тёрло, тёрли; отперéть/ óтпер, отперлá, óтперло, óтперли.

(b) Among verbs with infinitives ending in -нуть, most (e.g., крúк-нуть, "to shout") are regular (крúкнул, крúкнула, крúкнуло, крúк-нули), while a few (e.g., исчéзнуть,"to disappear") have the pattern исчéз, исчéзла, исчéзло, исчéзли.

(c) In most of the verb group with infinitives ending in -сти or -сть (вести, укрáсть, сесть, etc.), that whole ending is dropped before adding the past endings: вести/вёл, велá, велó, велú; укрáсть/ укрáл, укрáла, укрáло, укрáли; сесть/сел, сéла, сéло, сéли.

In two verbs, нести and трясти, the с of the infinitive is not dropped, and the masculine singular has no -л: нести/нёс, неслá, неслó, неслú; трясти/тряс, тряслá, тряслó, тряслú.

(d) In the verb group with infinitives ending in -зти or -зть (e.g., везти), the з is retained and the masculine singular has no -л: везти/вёз, везлá, везлó, везлú.

(e) In the verb group with infinitives ending in -чь (мочь, печь, лечь, etc.), the -чь is dropped and the г or к that appeared in the first person singular and third person plural of the present tense reappears here, too. The masculine singular has no -л, and in monosyllables e becomes ё: мочь/мог, могла́, могло́, могли́; печь/пёк, пекла́, пекло́, пекли́; лечь/лёг, легла́, легло́, легли́.

(f) The verb идти́ and the verbs derived from it by prefixes (e.g., прийти́) form their past tense from a completely different root: идти́/ шёл, шла, шло, шли; прийти́/пришёл, пришла́, пришло́, пришли́.

The past tense of грести́ is грёб, гребла́, гребло́, гребли́.

3. There are three possible stress patterns in the past tense: (a) stem stress in all four forms; (b) stress on the last syllable (when more than one) in all four forms; and (c) end stress in the feminine singular and stem stress in the other three forms. Examples: (a) говори́ть/говори́л, говори́ла, говори́ло, говори́ли; (b) нести́/нёс, несла́, несло́, несли́; (c) пить/пил, пила́, пи́ло, пи́ли.

Type (b) is frequent in verbs with infinitives that do not end in a vowel-plus-ть. Type (c) is typical of the group of verbs that begin with consonant clusters and have infinitives ending in -ать (ждать, врать, брать, звать, etc.); the group with infinitives ending in -нять (снять, приня́ть, etc.); and the group бить, пить, лить, etc.

THE FUTURE TENSE

The Future Tense of Perfective Verbs

The future tense of perfective verbs, which have no present tense, is formed in *exactly* the same way as the present tense of imperfective verbs. Thus, the Russian present tense in fact serves as a present/future tense: я **пишу́** [IMPF.] письмо́ ("I *am writing* a letter"); я **напишу́** [PF.] письмо́ ("I *shall write* a letter"); он **чита́ет** [IMPF.] кни́гу ("he *is reading* the book"); он **прочита́ет** [PF.] кни́гу ("he *will read* the book").

The Future Tense of Imperfective Verbs

Imperfective verbs have a separate compound future tense. This consists merely of the future tense of the verb быть ("to be")—бу́ду, бу́дешь, бу́дет, бу́дем, бу́дете, бу́дут—plus the infinitive of the imperfective verb in question. Thus: я **бу́ду чита́ть** кни́гу ("I *will read* the book," "I *will be reading* the book"); мы **бу́дем писа́ть** письмо́ ("we *shall write* the letter," "we *shall be writing* the letter"). There are no exceptions to this formation.

Naturally, the future tense of быть can be used independently to mean "will be": за́втра я бу́ду до́ма ("tomorrow I *will be* at home").

THE SUFFIX -СЯ; PASSIVE, REFLEXIVE AND INTRANSITIVE VERBS

1. The invariable suffix -ся (-сь after vowels), which causes no change in the conjugation of the main part of the verb, can do one of three things to a verb to which it is attached:

(a) It can make the verb passive (in this situation, the subject of the -ся verb is normally inanimate). Thus: стро́ить ("to build, construct, erect"); стро́иться ("to be built, constructed, erected").

Инжене́ры **стро́ят** но́вое зда́ние.
The engineers *are constructing* a new building.

Но́вое зда́ние **стро́ится** инжене́рами.
The new building *is being constructed* by the engineers.

As seen in **инжене́рами,** the agent of the action is in the instrumental case.

(b) It can make the verb reflexive. (In this situation, the subject of the -ся verb is almost always animate.) Thus: одева́ть ("to clothe, to dress someone else"), одева́ться ("to dress [oneself], to get dressed"); мыть ("to wash [something or someone]"), мы́ться ("to wash [oneself], to get washed").

Мать **одева́ет** ма́льчика.   The mother *is dressing* the little boy.
Ма́льчик **одева́ется.**   The little boy *is dressing (himself).*

Ле́на **посмотре́лась** в зе́ркало.
Lena *looked at herself* in the mirror.

Sometimes the action indicated by -ся is reciprocal (expressing "each other") rather than reflexive:

Они́ ча́сто **встреча́ются.**   They often *meet (each other).*
Они́ **ви́дятся** ка́ждый день.   They *see each other* every day.

(c) It can make the verb intransitive. (In this situation, the subject is generally animate, but not always.) Thus: ко́нчить ("to complete"), ко́нчиться ("to [come to an] end"); возвраща́ть ("to return [something]"), возвраща́ться ("to return [to a place]").

Я **ко́нчил** рабо́ту в пять часо́в.
I *finished* work at five o'clock.

Уро́к **ко́нчился** в два часа́.
The lesson *ended* at two o'clock.

Мы **возвраща́ем** кни́ги в библиоте́ку.
We *return* our books to the library.

Мы **возвраща́емся** в библиоте́ку.
We *return* to the library.

2. There are a few verbs that change their meaning more drastically when -ся is added; for instance:

слу́шать ("to listen")	слу́шаться ("to obey")
призна́ть ("to recognize")	призна́ться ("to confess")
состоя́ть ("to consist of")	состоя́ться ("to take place")

3. A number of verbs never occur without the suffix -ся, even if their English meaning does not seem to fit the above-mentioned situations. Some of the more important verbs of this kind are боро́ться ("to fight"), боя́ться ("to fear"), наде́яться ("to hope") and смея́ться ("to laugh"). The accusative case is never used for the direct object of such verbs.

4. There is an idiomatic use of -ся in which it is attached to the third person singular (neuter) form of the verb, and the logical subject of the verb is in the dative case:

Как **вам живётся**?   How's life treating you?

This construction lends a passive flavor to the expression, implying that the event is not controlled by you but happening to you whether you like it or not.

5. Naturally, Russian has numerous verbs that are purely intransitive (i.e., take no direct object at all in any grammatical case), and do not need the further addition of -ся. Such verbs include красне́ть ("to blush"), спеть ("to ripen"), идти́ ("to go") and па́дать ("to fall"). In some instances, the transitive and intransitive counterparts of a given action are expressed not by a single verb with and without -ся, but by two different (though often closely related) verbs. For instance:

TRANSITIVE	INTRANSITIVE
ве́сить ("to hang [something]")	висе́ть ("to hang [from something]")
жечь ("to burn [something]")	горе́ть ("to be aflame")
суши́ть ("to dry [something]")	со́хнуть ("to get dry")

IMPERSONAL CONSTRUCTIONS

1. There are a number of impersonal verbs in Russian that have only a third person singular form in the present tense. They usually refer to climatic conditions or other natural phenomena: светáет ("it is getting light"); смеркáется ("it is getting dark"). In the past tense, the neuter form is used: смеркáлось ("it was getting dark").

2. Some reflexive verbs can be used impersonally to express a physical state or feeling; they take the dative of the person to whom the action refers. The verb хотéться ("to want") is frequently used in this way:

Мне хóчется есть.	I feel hungry.
Емý хóчется пить.	He feels thirsty.
Брáту не рабóтается.	My brother doesn't feel like working.
Мне не спи́тся.	I don't feel sleepy.

3. Another important kind of impersonal construction that also involves the dative case is formed with the neuter short form of the adjective: мне хóлодно ("I am cold"); брáту жáрко ("my brother is hot"); емý скýчно ("he is bored").

4. There are a number of impersonal constructions expressing success or chance; here the person affected by the action is in the dative:

Мне удалóсь достáть билéт на «Лебеди́ное óзеро».
I succeeded in getting a ticket to "Swan Lake."

Брáту довелóсь поговори́ть с ним по телефóну.
My brother had occasion to talk to him on the telephone.

Брáту не везёт в кáрты.
My brother has no luck at cards.

5. The third person plural of a verb can be used (without the pronoun они́) in impersonal constructions. The unspecified agent of the verbal action is equivalent to the English "they," "one" or "people." It can often be rendered in English by a passive:

Говоря́т, что зáвтра дождь пойдёт.
They say that it will rain tomorrow.

Егó послáли на фронт.
They sent him [OR: He was sent] to the front.

EXPRESSING OBLIGATION, NECESSITY AND POSSIBILITY

1. Obligation is expressed in the present tense by using до́лжен ("must, ought, have to") followed by an infinitive (e.g., я до́лжен чита́ть э́ту кни́гу, "I must read this book"). До́лжен must agree in gender and number with its subject; its forms are: MASC. до́лжен, FEM. должна́, NEUT. должно́, PL. должны́. (Note that when the pronoun я or ты refers to a feminine subject then the form должна́ is used.) Thus:

Сего́дня она́ должна́ рабо́тать.
Today she must work.

Сего́дня мы должны́ рабо́тать.
Today we must work.

In forming the past and future tenses, до́лжен is used together with the appropriate form of the past or future tense of быть and the infinitive of the main verb:

Вчера́ я должна́ была́ рабо́тать.
Yesterday I had to work.

За́втра они́ должны́ бу́дут рабо́тать.
Tomorrow they will have to work.

2. Necessity is expressed in the present tense by using ну́жно or на́до ("it is necessary") followed by the infinitive (e.g., ну́жно пое́хать туда́, "it is necessary to go there"). In the past tense, ну́жно (or на́до) is used with бы́ло and an infinitive; in the future tense it is used with бу́дет and an infinitive:

Вчера́ ну́жно бы́ло пое́хать туда́.
Yesterday it was necessary to go there.

За́втра ну́жно бу́дет пое́хать туда́.
Tomorrow it will be necessary to go there.

Note the following difference in negative constructions between ну́жно and на́до:

Не ну́жно идти́ домо́й.	It is not necessary to go home.
Не на́до идти́ домо́й.	You should not go home.

3. Мо́жно is used to express possibility or permission; нельзя́ to express impossibility or prohibition:

Мо́жно реши́ть зада́чу.	It is possible to solve the problem.
Здесь мо́жно игра́ть.	One may play here.
Нельзя́ согласи́ться с ва́ми.	It is impossible to agree with you.
Здесь нельзя́ кури́ть.	It is not permitted to smoke here.

Both мо́жно and нельзя́ form the past and future tenses with бы́ло and бу́дет in the same way as ну́жно.

VERBS OF MOTION

In Russian there are 14 kinds of motion that are each expressed by two separate imperfective verbs. These imperfective pairs are: ходи́ть/идти́ ("to go," on foot); е́здить/е́хать ("to travel"); бе́гать/бежа́ть ("to run"); лета́ть/лете́ть ("to fly"); пла́вать/плыть ("to swim, float"); носи́ть/нести́ ("to carry"); води́ть/вести́ ("to lead"); вози́ть/везти́ ("to convey, transport"); ла́зить/лезть ("to climb"); гоня́ть/гнать ("to drive, chase"); таска́ть/тащи́ть ("to drag"); по́лзать/ползти́ ("to crawl"); ката́ть/кати́ть ("to roll"); броди́ть/брести́ ("to wander").

The first verb in each of the above pairs indicates habitual movement, movement in more than one direction, movement in general. Thus:

Пти́цы **лета́ют**, ры́ба **пла́вает**, лю́ди **хо́дят**.
Birds *fly*, fish *swim*, people *walk*.

Я люблю́ **е́здить** на маши́не.　　　I love *to ride* in the car.

The second verb in each of the above pairs indicates motion in one, often stipulated, direction, usually on one specific occasion:

Она́ **лети́т** в Москву́.　　　She *is flying* to Moscow.

Когда́ я **шёл** в шко́лу, я купи́л газе́ту.
When I *was on my way* to school, I stopped to buy a newspaper.

The perfective aspect of verbs of motion is formed by adding the prefix по- to the second verb of each pair (e.g., пойти́ [the contracted form of по + идти́], пое́хать, полете́ть, etc.). This prefix does not alter the imperfective meaning of the verb other than to imply the initiation of the action. Thus он пошёл means "he went," "he set out."

Compounded verbs of motion can be created to express direction by adding the appropriate prefix: (1) to the first verb in each of the pairs, thus creating an imperfective verb (e.g., приходи́ть, "to arrive"; входи́ть, "to enter"; вылета́ть, "to fly off"); or (2) to the second verb in each of the pairs, thus creating a perfective verb (e.g., придти́, "to arrive"; войти́, "to enter"; вы́лететь, "to fly off").

THE CONDITIONAL

The conditional mood expresses an action that might have taken place, that might be taking place or that might take place in the future. It is formed simply by using the past tense of the verb, imperfective or perfective, and the particle бы (sometimes б after a vowel). Thus: я пошёл бы ("I would go"). Note, however, that this construction can express not only the present conditional but the past and future conditional as well. Thus я пошёл бы can also mean "I would have gone" or "I would go (tomorrow)." Бы usually follows the verb, but can be placed elsewhere for emphasis: я бы пошёл ("*I* would go").

In a conditional sentence in which the main verb is in the conditional, the dependent clause is introduced by éсли бы and a verb in the past tense:

Éсли бы я не был так зáнят, я пошёл бы.
If I were not so busy I would go.

Éсли бы дождь пошёл, мы отменѝли бы матч.
If it were to rain we would cancel the game.

In a conditional sentence in which no genuine hypothesis is implied, then both clauses are in the indicative:

Éсли пойдёт дождь, мы отмéним матч.
If it rains we will cancel the game.

PARTICIPLES

Active Participles

Russian active participles are verbal adjectives, having the form of verbs but with adjectival endings (e.g., "The man *sitting* there is my friend," "The fire *burning* in the fields was started by accident"). Like adjectives, they are fully declinable and must agree in gender, number and case with the modified noun. There are two kinds of active participle in Russian: present and past. Present active participles can be formed only from imperfective verbs; past active participles can be formed from imperfective or perfective verbs.

The Present Active Participle. The present active participle is formed by taking the third person plural of the present tense of an imperfective verb, dropping the final -т of the personal ending and adding the adjectival ending: MASC. -щий, FEM. -щая, NEUT. -щее, PL. -щие. Thus the nominative forms of the present active participle of читáть (third person plural читáют) are читáющий, читáющая, читáющее and читáющие.

Present active participles are declined like those hard adjectives with stem ending in щ-. When a present active participle is formed from a verb with the -ся or -сь ending, the participle always takes -ся throughout: стрóиться ("to be built")/стрóящийся, стрóящаяся, стрóящееся, стрóящиеся. The stress in present active participles is usually the same as for the third person plural of the present tense.

The present active participle is used like an adjective to modify a noun; most often it is placed after the modified noun and replaces an entire relative clause. It is used when that clause would also be in the present tense if expressed. (It is important to note that Russian participles are never used as a complement to the verb "to be" as in English constructions such as "I am seeing," "we are doing.")

Мужчи́на, **иду́щий** по у́лице, мой оте́ц.
The man (*who is*) *going* down the street is my father.

Я не зна́ю мужчи́ну, **говоря́щего** с мои́м сосе́дом.
I don't know the man (*who is*) *talking* to my neighbor.

The Past Active Participle. The past active participle is formed by taking the masculine singular of the past tense of the verb (imperfective or perfective), dropping the final -л (if there is one) and adding -вший (-вшая, etc.). Thus the nominative forms of the past active participle of читáть (masc. sing. past читáл) are: MASC. читáвший, FEM. читáвшая, NEUT. читáвшее, PL. читáвшие; for the perfective verb прочитáть (masc. sing. past прочитáл) the forms are: MASC. прочитáвший, FEM. прочитáвшая, etc. The past active participle of reflexive verbs always ends in -ся.

The past active participle, which is declined and used like the present participle, usually replaces a relative clause that would be in the past tense if expressed:

Я прóдал биле́т мужчи́не, **стоя́вшему** на углу́.
I sold the ticket to the man (*who was*) *standing* on the corner.

Many active participles are also used as adjectives or nouns: блестя́щий ("brilliant"), соотве́тствующий ("appropriate"), куря́щий ("a smoker"), начина́ющий ("a beginner"), бы́вший ("former"), сумасше́дший ("a madman"), уцеле́вший ("a survivor").

Passive Participles

Like active participles, passive participles are also verbal adjectives (e.g., "The book *being read* is by Tolstoy," "The car *being driven* by my sister was green"). They are formed from verbs taking adjectival endings. Like adjectives, they are fully declinable and can be used attributively in the long form or predicatively in the short form. There are two kinds of passive participle: present and past. The present passive participle can only be formed from imperfective verbs; the past passive participle is for the most part formed from perfective verbs.

The Present Passive Participle. The present passive participle is formed by taking the first person plural of the present tense of a transitive imperfective verb and adding the adjectival ending: MASC. -ый, FEM. -ая, NEUT. -ое, PL. -ые. Thus the nominative forms of the present passive participle of читáть (first person plural читáем) are читáемый, читáемая, читáемое, читáемые. The only exceptions to this rule for forming the participle are: (1) verbs with infinitives ending -авáть, which take the participle form -авáемый, not -аёмый, (e.g., давáть/давáемый); and (2) a few verbs with first person plurals ending in -ём, in which the ё changes to о in the participle (e.g., вести́/ведóмый).

The stress in the participle is usually the same as in the first person plural of the present tense.

Many common verbs do not have any present passive participle; these include: (1) verbs with infinitives ending in -ерéть, -зть, -оть, -сть, -уть and -чь; and (2) many monosyllabic verbs (e.g., бить, брать, есть, ждать, звать, знать, лить, мыть, пить, петь).

The present active participle is declined like an adjective ending in -ый (e.g., краси́вый). The short form of the participle is the same as the short form of the adjective except that the stress remains the same as in the long form. Thus the short form of the present passive participle formed from читáть is читáем, читáема, читáемо, читáемы, etc. The present passive participle, which is used infrequently, can precede or follow the noun modified, and replaces a relative clause:

Кни́га, **читáемая** студéнтами, óчень скучнá.
The book (*that is*) *being read* by the students is very dull.

The Past Passive Participle. The past passive participle is more widely used than the present passive participle. It is formed in one of two ways: (1) with the suffix -т-; or (2) with the suffix -нн-.

1. Only a few verbs form their past passive participles with the -т- suffix. The participle is formed by replacing the infinitive ending -ть with the following endings: MASC. -тый, FEM. -тая, NEUT. -тое, PL. -тые. Verbs that form their past passive participle in this way include:

(a) Verbs with infinitives ending in -уть, -ыть, -оть or -ереть. Thus покинуть ("to abandon"), забыть ("to forget"), смолоть ("to grind") and запереть ("to lock") have the masculine nominative participle forms покинутый, забытый, смолотый and запертый (note that the second e is dropped in verbs ending in -ереть).

(b) Monosyllabic verbs (and their prefixed compounds) with infinitives ending in -ить or -еть. Thus одеть and убить have the past passive participle forms одетый and убитый.

(c) All verbs that introduce an н or м in the present tense conjugation. Thus взять, занять ("to crumple") and начать have the past passive participle forms взятый, занятый and начатый.

The short form of these participles resembles the short form of the adjective. Thus for одеть, the short forms of the nominative are: MASC. одет, FEM. одета, NEUT. одето, PL. одеты.

2. The vast majority of verbs form their past passive participle with the -нн- suffix. They take the participle endings: MASC. -нный, FEM. -нная, NEUT. -нное, PL. -нные. Verbs that belong to this group include:

(a) Conjugation I verbs with infinitives ending in -ать or -ять. These verbs replace the -ть of the infinitive with the ending -нный, (-нная, etc.) to form the participle. Thus прочитать and потерять have the past passive participle forms прочитанный and потерянный.

(b) Conjugation I verbs with infinitives ending in -сти or -зти. These verbs replace the -у of the first person singular of the present tense with the ending -ённый. Thus привести (first person singular приведу) and принести (first person singular принесу) have the past passive participle forms приведённый and принесённый.

(c) Conjugation I verbs with infinitives ending in -чь. These verbs replace the -ёшь of the second person singular of the present tense with the ending -ённый. Thus сжечь (second person singular сожжёшь) has the past passive participle сожжённый.

(d) Conjugation II verbs with infinitives ending in -ить or -еть. These verbs replace the -у or -ю of the first person singular of the present tense with -ённый (or -енный). Thus купить (first person singular куплю) and решить (first person singular решу) have the past passive participle forms купленный and решённый.

The short form of participles ending in -нный differs from the usual adjectival short form in that it drops one н. Thus the short form of прочи́танный is прочи́тан, прочи́тана, прочи́тано, прочи́таны.

There are no straightforward guidelines to stress in the past passive participles. Only a rudimentary analysis can be provided here:

(a) In verbs with infinitives ending in -уть, -оть or -ере́ть, and in verbs like нача́ть, the stress in the participle moves one syllable back from its position in the infinitive (e.g., нача́ть/на́чатый).

(b) In verbs with a past passive participle ending in -анный or -янный the stress falls on the syllable preceding the -a- or -я- of the ending (e.g., прочи́танный, поте́рянный).

(c) In Conjugation II verbs with a past passive participle ending in -енный or -ённый the stress is the same as in the second person singular of the present tense. Thus: ку́пленный (second person singular ку́пишь); решённый (second person singular реши́шь).

The past passive participle can be used to replace a relative clause as an attribute of a noun (with which it must agree in gender, case and number). Used attributively, the participle must be in the long form.

Этот мост, **постро́енный** инжене́рами, о́чень кре́пкий.
This bridge (*that was*) *built* by the engineers is very strong.

The past passive participle can also be used (in the short form only) as a complement to the verb быть:

Мой брат был **уби́т** во вре́мя войны́.
My brother was *killed* during the war.

GERUNDS

Russian gerunds are verbal adverbs corresponding to English verbal forms ending in "-ing" (e.g., "reading," "writing," "walking"), but are distinguished from participles in that they never describe nouns; instead they describe actions. For instance, in the sentence "She sits reading," the word "reading" would be rendered in Russian by the gerund чита́я. There are two kinds of gerund in Russian: present gerund and past gerund. Both present and past gerunds are indeclinable.

Formation of the Present Gerund

The present gerund is formed by taking the present tense stem of an imperfective verb and adding the ending -я (or -a if the stem ends in ж-, ч-, ш- or щ-. Thus the present gerunds of читáть and дышáть ("to breathe") are читáя ("reading") and дышá ("breathing"). Verbs with infinitives ending in -авáт are the only exception to the above rule; they take the ending -авáя (e.g., давáя, "giving"). The present gerund of reflexive verbs always takes the reflexive ending -сь (e.g., смея́сь, "laughing"). Stress in the present gerund is the same as in the first person singular of the present tense.

Many Russian verbs do not have a present gerund. These include: (a) the common verbs бежáть, бить, врать, гнить, есть, éхать, ждать, лезть, лить, петь, писáть, пить, слать, хотéть, шить; (b) verbs ending in -ерéть; (c) verbs ending in -нуть.

Formation of the Past Gerund

The past gerund is formed almost exclusively from perfective verbs. Perfective verbs with a masculine singular past tense ending in -л drop the -л and add the ending -в (or sometimes -вши) to form the past gerund. Thus the past gerunds of the perfective verbs прочитáть and поговори́ть are прочитáв ("having read") and поговори́в ("having said"). Reflexive verbs take the ending -вшись (e.g., верну́вшись, "having returned"). For verbs with no -л in the masculine singular past tense, the past gerund is formed by adding the ending -ши to the masculine singular form of the past tense. Thus the past gerunds of принести́ (masc. sing. past при́нёс) and вы́лезть (masc. sing. past вы́лез) are принёсши ("having brought") and вы́лезши ("having climbed out"). The forms ending in -ши are not common and are usually replaced by a present gerund formed from the perfective verb.

Use of the Gerund

Gerunds are used to describe an action or to modify a previous verb; they cannot be used as participles to describe a noun. Thus the gerund replaces a clause consisting of a verb and conjunction. The sentence "she sits *and reads*" can be rendered using a present gerund as онá сиди́т, **читáя**.

The present gerund is used to describe an action that occurs at the same time as the action expressed by the main verb, irrespective of the tense (past, present, future) or aspect of that verb:

Смея́сь и **улыбáясь**, дéти слу́шают бáсню.
Laughing and *smiling*, the children listen to the fable.

Смея́сь и **улыба́ясь**, де́ти слу́шали ба́сню.
Laughing and *smiling*, the children listened to the fable.

The past gerund is usually used to express an action that precedes the action expressed by the main verb, irrespective of the tense or aspect of that verb:

Напи́вшись, путеше́ственники на́чали расска́зывать о свои́х приключе́ниях.
Having drunk their fill, the travelers began to relate their adventures.

There are a number of gerunds that have taken on the value of prepositions and adverbs. These include благодаря́ + dat. ("thanks to"), исключа́я + gen. ("except for, excluding"), конча́я + instr. ("ending with"), начина́я с + gen. ("beginning with"), несмотря́ на + acc. ("in spite of, despite"), мо́лча ("silently"), не́хотя ("unwillingly").

VERBAL PREFIXES

Prefixes are an important element of numerous Russian verbs, imperfective as well as perfective. Except when the only use of a prefix is to transform an imperfective into a perfective (e.g., чита́ть into прочита́ть), it usually has a specific meaning or set of meanings that alter the basic meaning of the verb accordingly. In the following list of common prefixes, it will be obvious how many correspond to prepositions, often with exactly the same meanings (these prefixes also occur on many nouns and adjectives with similar connotations).

PREFIX	VERB WITHOUT PREFIX	VERB WITH PREFIX
в- (во-; "into")	ходи́ть ("to go")	входи́ть ("to enter")
вз- (воз-, вс-; "upward")	лете́ть ("to fly")	взлете́ть ("to fly up, take off")
вы- ("out of")	води́ть ("to lead")	выводи́ть ("to lead out")
до- ("up to, to the end")	чита́ть ("to read")	дочита́ть ("to read up to [a certain point]")
за- ("behind, beyond"; beginning of an action; filling up)	пусти́ть ("to let go")	запусти́ть ("to launch")
	молча́ть ("to be silent")	замолча́ть ("to fall silent")
	стро́ить ("to build")	застро́ить ("to build up [an area]")
из- (ис-; "out; completely")	брать ("to take")	избра́ть ("to pick out, choose")
	писа́ть ("to write")	исписа́ть ("to cover with writing")

на- ("on, onto; a lot")	пада́ть ("to fall")	напада́ть ("to fall upon, attack")
	пить ("to drink")	напи́ть ("to drink a lot")
над- ("over")	писа́ть ("to write")	надписа́ть ("to superscribe, endorse")
о- (об-; "around, about")	éхать ("to drive")	объéхать ("to detour")
от- (ото-; "away from; back")	ходи́ть ("to go")	отходи́ть ("to move away from")
	дава́ть ("to give")	отдава́ть ("to give back")
пере- ("across, through; again; over and above")	жить ("to live")	пережи́ть ("to experience")
	чита́ть ("to read")	перечита́ть ("to reread")
	выполня́ть ("to fulfill")	перевыполня́ть ("to overfulfill")
по- ("for a while"; beginning of an action)	сиде́ть ("to sit")	посиде́ть ("to sit for a while")
	люби́ть ("to love")	полюби́ть ("to start to love")
под- ("under; toward")	держа́ть ("to hold")	поддержа́ть ("to support")
	ходи́ть ("to go")	подходи́ть ("to approach")
пред- ("pre-")	сказа́ть ("to tell")	предсказа́ть ("to foretell")
при- ("coming to; getting used to")	ходи́ть ("to go")	приходи́ть ("to arrive")
про- ("through, by, past")	ходи́ть ("to go")	проходи́ть ("to pass by")
раз- ("apart; un-")	бить ("to hit")	разби́ть ("to break into bits")
	люби́ть ("to love")	разлюби́ть ("to cease to love")
с- (со-; "downward; off")	ходи́ть ("to go")	сходи́ть ("to come down, go off")
у- ("away from")	брать ("to take")	убра́ть ("to take away")

When certain prefixes are added to verbs in conjunction with the suffix -ся, special connotations are generated:

1. When the verb has the prefix до- and the suffix -ся, the implication is successful completion of the basic meaning: звони́ть ("to call up"), дозвони́ться ("to reach by telephone, to complete the call").

2. With the prefix за- and the suffix -ся, the implication is excessive action that causes a loss of control: мечта́ть ("to daydream"), замечта́ться ("to become lost in daydreams").

3. With the prefix на- and the suffix -ся, the implication is action done to satiety: пить ("to drink"), **напи́ться** ("to drink one's fill").

4. With the prefix о- and the suffix -ся, the implication is the incorrect performance of the verb action: ступа́ть ("to take a step"), **оступа́ться** ("to stumble").

5. With the prefix раз- and the suffix -ся, the implication is sudden, intense action: горе́ть ("to burn"), **разгоре́ться** ("to blaze up suddenly").

6. With the prefix с- and the suffix -ся, the implication is convergence on a single point: брать ("to take"), **собра́ться** ("to assemble").

VERBS: ASPECT

We have already seen that most Russian verbs occur in imperfective/perfective aspectival pairs, distinguished by prefixing, difference in conjugational endings or alteration in the stem; sometimes two completely different verbs are used to form the pair. We have also seen that, in simplest terms, imperfective verbs describe uncompleted actions, and perfective verbs describe actions that have been or will be completed. It is now time to elaborate on the use of the two aspects. It should be borne in mind that, in any verb pair, the role played by aspect is closely connected with the kind of action denoted. Of course, there are many subtle rules of aspect that cannot be given here. Mastery of all the niceties of aspect requires long personal experience of the language. (In this chapter, whenever aspectival pairs are separated by a slash [/], the imperfective precedes the perfective.)

BASIC DIFFERENCES BETWEEN IMPERFECTIVE AND PERFECTIVE

1. Imperfective verbs denote:
(a) Generic action (no reference to a specific performance of the action):

Неда́вно я научи́лся **пла́вать**.   Not long ago I learned *to swim*.

(b) Action in progress (any tense):

Сейча́с он **разгова́ривает** с тётей.
Right now he *is talking* with his aunt.

Она́ **чита́ла** кни́гу, когда́ я вошёл в ко́мнату.
She *was reading* a book when I entered the room.

Я бу́ду рабо́тать всю ночь над э́тим.
I *will be working* all night on this.

(c) Repeated or habitual action (any tense):

Ка́ждое у́тро он **пьёт** ко́фе.   Every morning he *drinks* coffee.

В де́тстве я ча́сто **е́здил** верхо́м.
In my childhood I often *rode* on horseback.

С э́тих пор я ра́но **бу́ду встава́ть**.
From now on I *will get up* early.

The imperfective is also used in questions when one wants to know merely whether or not an action took place, or who is responsible for an action that has taken place:

Вы **чита́ли** «Мёртвые ду́ши»?   Have you *read* "Dead Souls"?

One subtle use of the imperfective (of certain verbs, in the past tense only) is to show that a given action was done and then undone—for instance, that a window was opened and then closed again:

Кто **открыва́л** [IMPF.] окно́?
Who *opened* the window (and then closed it again)?

Кто **откры́л** [PF.] окно́?
Who *opened* the window (and left it open)?

2. Perfective verbs delimit the action. They denote:
(a) Action that is carried through from beginning to end:

Я **прочита́л** э́ту кни́гу за три неде́ли.
I *read through* this book in three weeks.

(b) A single, instantaneous action:

Учи́тель **уда́рил** по столу́.
The teacher *gave a rap* on his desk.

(c) The very beginning of an action:

Де́вочка **закрича́ла**, когда́ она́ уви́дела медве́дя.
The girl *began to shriek* when she caught sight of the bear.

(d) Action performed for a short while:

Он **посиде́л** и **почита́л**.   He *sat for a while* and *read a bit*.

When a specific action is to be completed, even though it is to be repeated in a series, as in "*Write* this word a hundred times," the perfective is used (i.e., напиши́те, not пиши́те) because the idea of the completion of the action is the stronger element.

ASPECT AND NEGATION

1. When an action is being completely negated, an imperfective verb is used (even when the positive action would be in the perfective aspect):

POSITIVE:

Я вам сове́тую **написа́ть** [PF.] ему́.
I advise you *to write* to him.

NEGATIVE:

Я вам сове́тую не **писа́ть** [IMPF.] ему́.
I advise you not *to write* to him.

This is because the action in general is being denied, prevented or negated. When the negated verb is perfective, the implication is that the action was undertaken but never completed:

Я **не чита́л** [IMPF.] э́ту кни́гу.   I *haven't read* that book (at all).
Я **не прочита́л** [PF.] э́ту кни́гу.   I *haven't read* that book *through*.

2. If the degree of negation is not total, the attitude of the speaker is a determining factor as to which aspect is used. If the action being denied or negated was never expected to happen, the imperfective is used:

Я **не получа́л** письма́ сего́дня.
I *didn't get* any letter today [but wasn't expecting one].

If the negated action is still expected to take place, either aspect can be used:

Я ещё **не получа́л/получи́л** све́дений.
I *have not* yet *received* news [but I expect some].

If an action was expected, but never took place, the perfective is used:

Я до́лго ждал, но он так и **не пришёл**.
I waited a long time but he *didn't come*.

If the absence of an action continues for some time, the imperfective is used:

Мы давно́ **не ви́делись**.
We *haven't seen each other* for some time.

All of the above situations shed light on a basic distinction between the two aspects: the imperfective verb is more general than the perfective. Accordingly, its negation is more sweeping and far-reaching. Perfective verbs always refer to a specific situation or set of conditions.

ASPECT OF INFINITIVES AND IMPERATIVES

1. There are instances when infinitives must be of a particular aspect. They must be imperfective:

(a) After verbs of beginning, continuing and ceasing (because those very verbs already provide the limitation of the action):

Вчера́ она́ начала́ **чита́ть** «Идио́та».
Yesterday she started *to read* "The Idiot."

(b) After verbs of learning and becoming accustomed (because the reference is to the action of the infinitive in general):

Он привы́к **исполня́ть** свои́ обеща́ния.
He is accustomed *to keep* his promises.

After perfective verbs that refer to a single instance, the infinitive must be perfective:

Я забы́л **оста́вить** ключ на столе́.
I forgot *to leave* the key on the table.

When the main verb of the sentence is imperfective, the infinitive can be of either aspect:

Я всегда́ забыва́ю **оставля́ть/оста́вить** ключ на столе́.
I always forget *to leave* the key on the table.

2. The imperative, like the verb in general, uses the perfective when referring to a single, defined action. Thus, "open the window!"is normally откро́йте окно́! The use of the imperfective here would express exasperated impatience: открыва́йте уже́ ("get a move on and open it!"). However, verbs of invitation are usually in the imperfective and the perfective would be considered rude. Thus: сади́тесь! ("have a seat!"), входи́те! ("come in!"), приходи́те! ("come over!"), etc., are all imperfectives.

In negative imperatives, the imperfective is normally used even if a single, instantaneous action is being referred to: не по́йте э́ту пе́сню! ("don't sing that song!"). When the negative perfective is used, it is with the connotation "be careful not to . . . in order to avoid bad consequences." Thus: не забу́дьте! ("don't forget!").

STRUCTURAL RELATIONS BETWEEN IMPERFECTIVES AND PERFECTIVES

1. Some of the structural differences between imperfective and perfective verbs have already been mentioned. The perfective verb may have a prefix that the imperfective does not have: чита́ть/**про**чита́ть ("to read"), писа́ть/**на**писа́ть ("to write"), шить/**с**шить ("to sew"), etc. The vowels of the endings may differ: конча́ть/ко́нчить ("to finish"), уменьшáть/умéньшить ("to decrease"), решáть/решúть ("to decide"). But there are numerous other variations in these structural differences between the two aspects, and until one has learned enough pairs to recognize patterns, there is no reliable way of predicting the structure of a given verb's counterpart.

Generally speaking, the two members of an imperfective/perfective verb pair differ in meaning solely with regard to aspect. Thus, писáть and написáть, its perfective partner, both have the basic meaning "to write." But, as we have seen, prefixes can change the basic meaning: **переписáть** ("to rewrite"), **вы́писать** ("to delete"), **подписáть** ("to sign"), **прописáть** ("to prescribe"), etc. This type of verb—formed by the addition of prefixes directly to the original verb—is always perfective, and the differences in meaning between those with the same base is derived solely from the prefixes.

2. (a) Since these newly formed prefixed verbs are perfective, they must have imperfective counterparts that retain the meaningful prefixes. The changes that distinguish the aspects must thus appear in the endings, in the main stems or in both. For example, the imperfective corresponding to переписáть is перепи́сывать; the imperfective corresponding to перечитáть ("to reread") is перечи́тывать. The other -писать and -читать verbs do the same. These are just some of the verbs in which the imperfective differs from the perfective by having -ыв- inserted into it. Examples of other possible structural relations follow:

(b) The element -ва- inserted in the imperfective: одевáть/одéть ("to dress"), открывáть/откры́ть ("to open"), отставáть/отстáть ("to fall behind").

(c) The element -ин- inserted in the imperfective: начинáть/начáть ("to begin").

(d) The vowel -и- or -ы- inserted in the imperfective: избирáть/избрáть ("to choose"), посылáть/послáть ("to send").

(e) The alternation of -ать (or -ять) in the imperfective with -ить in the perfective infinitive (with consequent alternation of personal endings between Conjugation I and Conjugation II): бросáть/брóсить ("to throw"; an instance of a verb pair in which neither has a prefix), получáть/получи́ть ("to receive"), изменя́ть/измени́ть ("to change"), исполня́ть/испóлнить ("to fulfill").

(f) In some instances of the -ять/-ить alternation, -л- is also inserted in the imperfective. (This is analogous to the -л- inserted in the first person singular—люблю́—of such verbs as люби́ть.) Thus: представля́ть/предстáвить ("to introduce").

(g) Other types of consonant mutation may occur in the -ать/-ить pairs: отвечáть/отвéтить ("to answer"), прекращáть/прекрати́ть ("to

discontinue"), проща́ться/прости́ться ("to say goodbye"), пригла-
ша́ть/пригласи́ть ("to invite").

(h) In some verbs, the -ать/-ить alternation is combined with the
insertion in the imperfective of -ыв- or -ив- (sometimes also involving the
insertion of -л-, consonant mutation and/or an а/о alternation in stem
vowels): остана́вливать/останови́ть ("to stop"), сосредото́чи-
вать/сосредото́чить ("to concentrate"), спра́шивать/спроси́ть ("to
ask").

(i) Another alternation, -ать/-нуть, can involve consonant mutation and
changes in the stem vowel: стиха́ть/сти́хнуть ("to become quiet"),
крича́ть/кри́кнуть ("to shout, cry out"), отдыха́ть/отдохну́ть ("to
rest"). With almost no exceptions, -нуть verbs indicate that the action takes
place instantaneously and just once; thus, кри́кнуть means "to utter a
single shout or cry."

(j) The perfective -нять verbs have -нима́ть imperfectives: снима́ть/
снять ("to take away").

3. To generalize about identifying a given verb as being imperfective or
perfective:

(a) When one verb in an aspectival pair has a prefix and the other does
not, the prefixed one is almost always perfective. When both verbs have
prefixes, the longer of the two is likely to be the imperfective.

(b) Verbs with infinitives ending in -ывать, -вать or -ать tend to be
imperfective, and those ending in -ить are often perfective.

(c) When there is an alternation between а and о in the stem of a verb
pair, the one with the а is likely to be imperfective and the one with the о
perfective.

4. In addition to all the above-mentioned instances of structural alternations
between imperfective and perfective verbs, there are a number of pairs in
which the verbs are totally different. These include: брать/взять ("to
take"), лови́ть/пойма́ть ("to catch"), класть/положи́ть ("to place,
put"), говори́ть/сказа́ть ("to speak, say, tell").

When prefixes are added to the verbs, the tendency is for only one form
out of the unprefixed pair to be used as the basic of both the imperfective and
the perfective of the new prefixed pair (structural changes of the above-
mentioned types are also involved). The member of the unprefixed pair that
is usually chosen is the imperfective one. Thus, the prefixed verbs formed
from the брать/взять pair are отбира́ть/отобра́ть ("to take away"),
набира́ть/набра́ть ("to gather"), etc. A prefixed verb formed from the
лови́ть/пойма́ть pair is ула́вливать/улови́ть ("to seize, grasp"). On
the other hand, the класть/положи́ть pair retains both forms, in the
appropriate aspects, when prefixes are added: укла́дывать/уложи́ть

("to pack, put away"), откла́дывать/отложи́ть ("to postpone"), etc. The говори́ть/сказа́ть pair forms new prefixed verbs with the same form as the base of both imperfective and perfective, but some of the new prefixed verbs use говори́ть and some use сказа́ть. Thus: угова́ривать/уговори́ть ("to persuade"), отгова́ривать/отговори́ть ("to dissuade"); выска́зывать/вы́сказать ("to express"), расска́зывать/рассказа́ть ("to relate").

ASPECTIVAL PAIRS OF AN ATTEMPT/SUCCEED NATURE

Although the two members of aspectival pairs generally have the same meaning (except with regard to aspect), there are a number of important verbs whose imperfectives indicate an attempt to achieve a certain goal, and whose perfectives denote the successful attainment of the goal or completion of the action. Examples are:

IMPERFECTIVE	PERFECTIVE
буди́ть ("to try to awaken")	разбуди́ть ("to awaken")
добива́ться ("to try to obtain")	доби́ться ("to obtain")
дока́зывать ("to try to prove")	доказа́ть ("to prove")
лови́ть ("to try to catch")	пойма́ть ("to catch")
объясня́ть ("to try to explain")	объясни́ть ("to explain")
реша́ть ("to try to solve")	реши́ть ("to solve")
убежда́ть ("to try to convince")	убеди́ть ("to convince")
угова́ривать ("to try to persuade")	уговори́ть ("to persuade")

Examples of usage:

Мили́ция до́лго **лови́ла** его́ и в конце́ концо́в **пойма́ла**.
The police *tried to catch* him for a long time and finally *did* (*catch* him).

Она́ **буди́ла** и **буди́ла**, но не **разбуди́ла** его́.
She *tried* and *tried* (*to wake* him), but she *could*n't *wake* him up.

Since perfectives have no present tense, the imperfectives of these verb pairs can be used to denote success in the present:

Ка́ждое у́тро мать его́ **бу́дит**.
His mother *wakes* him *up* every morning.

TELLING TIME

There are two ways in which to ask "What time is it?" in Russian: Котóрый час? or, colloquially, Скóлько врéмени? The answer, when indicating a time on the hour, is expressed using cardinal numbers and the word час (час is in the genitive singular when preceded by два, "two"; три, "three"; or четы́ре "four"; in the genitive plural when preceded by the other numbers): два часá ("two o'clock"), три часá ("three o'clock"), пять часóв ("five o'clock"). "One o'clock" is simply час.

Half hours are expressed using половúна ("half") and the genitive masculine singular of the ordinal of the following hour: половúна трéтьего ("half past two"), половúна четвёртого ("half past three").

"Quarter past" is expressed using чéтверть and the genitive masculine singular of the ordinal of the following hour: чéтверть трéтьего ("quarter past two"), чéтверть четвёртого ("quarter past three").

Minutes past the hour are expressed using cardinal numbers plus минýта (in the genitive, singular or plural) and the genitive masculine singular of the ordinal of the following hour for the hour: пять минýт одúннадцатого ("five minutes past ten"), двáдцать минýт шестóго ("twenty minutes past five").

Minutes to the hour are expressed using the preposition без plus the number of minutes (in the genitive) and the nominative of the cardinal number for the hour: без десятú шесть ("ten to six"), без чéтверти пять ("quarter to five").

To express "at [a given hour]" the preposition в is used with the accusative of the hour: в час ("at one o'clock"), в три часá ("at three o'clock"). Note that в is not used with без; thus без десятú шесть can mean "ten to six" or "at ten to six" as the context requires.

USEFUL EXPRESSIONS

Listed below are some useful expressions that have not appeared in the main body of this grammar:

Пожа́луйста.	Please.
Спаси́бо.	Thank you.
Мо́жет быть.	Perhaps.
Здра́вствуй(те).	How do you do?
До свида́ния.	Good-bye.
До́брое у́тро.	Good morning.
До́брый ве́чер.	Good evening.
Споко́йной но́чи.	Good night.
Поздравля́ю.	Congratulations.
Как вы пожива́ете?	How are you?
О́чень хорошо́, а как вы?	Very well, and you?
Хорошо́.	All right.
Извини́те.	Excuse me.
О́чень прия́тно.	Pleased to meet you.
Как ва́ше и́мя?	What is your (first) name?
Моё и́мя...	My name is...
Как ва́ша фами́лия?	What is your surname?
Вы говори́те по-англи́йски?	Do you speak English?
Пожа́луйста, говори́те ме́дленнее.	Please speak more slowly.
Как по-ру́сски...?	What is Russian for...?
Я не понима́ю.	I don't understand.
Ско́лько э́то сто́ит?	How much does this cost?
Я хочу́ есть/пить.	I am hungry/thirsty.

APPENDIX I: SPECIAL NOUN DECLENSIONS AND IRREGULAR NOUNS

MASCULINE NOUNS

1. The word брат ("brother") has the following plural: NOM. бра́тья, ACC. бра́тьев, GEN. бра́тьев, DAT. бра́тьям, INSTR. бра́тьями, PREP. бра́тьях. Similarly declined in the plural (except that, as inanimates, their accusative is like their nominative, not like their genitive) are стул ("chair") and лист ("leaf"). (Note that when лист means "sheet of paper" it has the regular plural: NOM. листы́, GEN. листо́в, etc.)

2. The word муж ("husband") has the plural: NOM. мужья́, ACC. муже́й, GEN. муже́й, DAT. мужья́м, INSTR. мужья́ми, PREP. мужья́х. The word князь ("prince") is declined in the same way in the plural, as is друг ("friend"), except that the г of друг changes to з: князья́, князе́й, etc.; друзья́, друзе́й, etc. Similar is сын ("son"), except that -ов- is inserted between stem and endings: сыновья́, сынове́й, etc.

3. A few masculine nouns have a genitive plural that is the same as the nominative singular: глаз ("eye"), солда́т ("soldier"), сапо́г ("boot"), боти́нок ("shoe"), чуло́к ("stocking"), челове́к ("person"), раз ("time," as in "one more time"). There is a shift in stress in во́лос ("hair," nom. sing.)/воло́с (gen. pl.).

4. In both singular and plural, the word путь ("way, road") is declined like the feminine nouns that end in -ь: NOM. путь, GEN. пути́, etc., except that the stress is always on the endings and the instrumental singular is путём.

5. A small group of masculine nouns, usually referring to a national or social group of people, end in -анин or -янин in the nominative singular. The singular is always regular: граждани́н ("citizen"), граждани́ну, граждани́на, etc.; крестья́нин ("peasant"), крестья́нину, крестья́нина, etc. The plural of граждани́н is: NOM. гра́ждане, ACC. гра́ждан, GEN. гра́ждан, DAT. гра́жданам, INSTR. гра́жданами, PREP. гра́жданах. The plural of крестья́нин is: NOM. крестья́не, ACC. крестья́н, GEN. крестья́н, DAT. крестья́нам, INSTR. крестья́нами, PREP. крестья́нах. Declined like граждани́н (aside from stress) are such words as христиа́нин ("Christian") and персиа́нин ("Persian"). Declined like крестья́нин (aside from stress) are армяни́н ("Armenian") and славяни́н ("Slav"). The feminine counterparts of -анин/-янин masculines— such as гражда́нка ("woman citizen") and крестья́нка ("peasant woman")—are regular in declension.

6. Nouns with nominative singulars ending in -онок or -ёнок denote the young of human beings or animals: ребёнок ("baby, child"), котёнок ("kitten"), медвежо́нок ("bear cub"), etc. They are regular in the singular: NOM. котёнок, ACC. котёнка, GEN. котёнка, DAT. котёнку, INSTR. котёнком, PREP. котёнке. They have the plural pattern: NOM. котя́та, ACC. котя́т, GEN. котя́т, DAT. котя́там, INSTR. котя́тами, PREP. котя́тах. Exception: щено́к ("puppy"), with the plural щенки́, щенко́в, etc.

FEMININE NOUNS

1. The word мать ("mother") is declined:

	SINGULAR	PLURAL
NOM.	мать	ма́тери
ACC.	мать	матере́й
GEN.	ма́тери	матере́й
DAT.	ма́тери	матеря́м
INSTR.	ма́терью	матеря́ми
PREP.	ма́тери	матеря́х

The word дочь ("daughter") is declined in the same way—дочь, дочь, до́чери, etc.—except for the instrumental plural, which is дочерьми́.

2. Though most feminines with nominative singulars ending in -я preceded by a consonant have a genitive plural ending in -ь (неде́ля/неде́ль), the genitive plural of -ня feminines usually ends in -ен: пе́сня ("song"), GEN. PL. пе́сен. However, дере́вня ("countryside") and ку́хня ("kitchen") are regular, the genitive plurals being дереве́нь and ку́хонь.

NEUTER NOUNS

1. The small but important group of neuters with nominative singulars ending in -мя (e.g., вре́мя, "time") are declined as follows:

	SINGULAR	PLURAL
NOM.	вре́мя	времена́
ACC.	вре́мя	времена́
GEN.	вре́мени	времён
DAT.	вре́мени	времена́м
INSTR.	вре́менем	времена́ми
PREP.	вре́мени	времена́х

Others in this group are бре́мя ("burden"), зна́мя ("banner"), и́мя ("name"), пла́мя ("flame"), пле́мя ("tribe") and се́мя ("seed"). The only one that deviates at all in declension is зна́мя, which has the plural: NOM. знамёна, ACC. знамёна, GEN. знамён, DAT. знамёнам, INSTR. знамёнами, PREP. знамёнах.

2. The word чу́до ("miracle, wonder") has the plural: NOM. чудеса́, ACC. чудеса́, GEN. чуде́с, DAT. чудеса́м, INSTR. чудеса́ми, PREP. чудеса́х. Declined in the same way is не́бо ("sky"), which means "heavens" in the plural: NOM. небеса́, ACC. небеса́, GEN. небе́с, etc.

3. A number of neuters have other irregularities in the plural; only a few common ones are mentioned here. The word де́рево ("tree") has the plural: NOM. дере́вья, ACC. дере́вья, GEN. дере́вьев, DAT. дере́вьям, INSTR. дере́вьями, PREP. дере́вьях. Declined like де́рево are крыло́ ("wing")—кры́лья, кры́лья, кры́льев, etc.—and перо́ ("feather")—пе́рья, пе́рья, пе́рьев, etc. The word я́блоко ("apple") is irregular only in the nominative and accusative plural: я́блоки. The words пла́тье ("dress") and о́блако ("cloud") are irregular in the genitive plural only: пла́тьев, облако́в. The word коле́но ("knee") has the plural: коле́ни, коле́ни, коле́ней, etc. The word у́хо ("ear") has the plural: у́ши, у́ши, уше́й, etc.

APPENDIX II: DECLENSION OF NUMERALS

CARDINAL NUMERALS

1. Оди́н ("one") must agree in gender, number and case with the noun it precedes; a noun modified by оди́н is always in the singular unless it is a plural-only noun. The nominative forms of оди́н are: MASC. оди́н, FEM. одна́, NEUT. одно́, PL. одни́. (The -и- appears only in the nominative singular.) Thus: оди́н стол ("one table"); одна́ кни́га ("one book"); одно́ окно́ ("one window"); одни́ часы́ ("one clock"). Оди́н declines like э́тот, except that the stress is on the ending.

Оди́н can also have the meaning "alone": я оди́н (OR: одна́) зна́ю ("I alone know"); они́ пришли́ одни́ ("they came alone").

2. Два ("two") has two forms in the nominative and inanimate accusative: MASC. & NEUT. два, FEM. две. Both три ("three") and четы́ре ("four") have only one nominative form. They are declined thus:

NOM.	два (две)	три	четы́ре
ACC.	два (две)	три	четы́ре
(ANIM.)	двух	трёх	четырёх
GEN.	двух	трёх	четырёх
DAT.	двум	трём	четырём
INSTR.	двумя́	тремя́	четырьмя́
PREP.	двух	трёх	четырёх

These three numerals, when in the nominative or accusative (except when referring to human beings), are followed by nouns in the genitive singular. Thus: два стола́ ("two tables"); две кни́ги ("two books"); три соба́ки ("three dogs"). In the accusative, when referring to human beings (but not animals), and in the other cases the noun takes the same case as the numeral and is in the plural.

3. О́ба ("both") has two gender-indicating forms: MASC. & NEUT. о́ба, FEM. о́бе. О́ба is declined thus:

	MASC. & NEUT.	FEM.
NOM.	óба	óбе
ACC.	óба	óбе
(ANIM.)	обóих	обéих
GEN.	обóих	обéих
DAT.	обóим	обéим
INSTR.	обóими	обéими
PREP.	обóих	обéих

Óба (óбе) follows the same rules as those governing два (две).

4. Пять ("five") is declined: NOM./ACC. пять, GEN./DAT./PREP. пяти́, INSTR. пятью́. Шесть ("six") through два́дцать ("twenty"), and три́дцать ("thirty") are declined like пять. (Note, however, that the -e- in вóсемь ["eight"] is replaced by -ь- in the genitive, dative and prepositional cases.) All these numerals follow the same rules as those for два, except that they are followed by the genitive plural when in the nominative and accusative. The nominative and accusative of all numerals from 5–999 are followed by the genitive plural.

5. Compound numerals are formed as in English, except that no hyphen or conjunction is used. Thus: два́дцать четы́ре ("twenty-four"). Nouns modified by compound numerals are governed by the last element.

6. Сóрок ("forty") has an accusative form identical to the nominative. In all the other cases it takes the ending -a (сорокá). Девянóсто ("ninety") and сто ("hundred") are both declined like сóрок. Thus their genitives are девянóста and ста.

7. In each of the numerals from пятьдеся́т ("fifty") to вóсемьдесят ("eighty") both elements decline. Thus пятьдеся́т declines: NOM./ACC. пятьдеся́т, GEN./DAT./PREP. пяти́десяти, INSTR. пятью́десятью.

8. Both elements decline in the numerals двéсти ("two hundred") through девятьсóт ("nine hundred"); note that the сто element is declined as a plural:

NOM.	двéсти	три́ста	пятьсóт
ACC.	двéсти	три́ста	пятьсóт
GEN.	двухсóт	трёхсóт	пятисóт
DAT.	двумстáм	трёмстáм	пятистáм
INSTR.	двумястáми	тремястáми	пятьюстáми
PREP.	двухстáх	трёхстáх	пятистáх

9. Тысяча ("thousand") and миллио́н ("million") are both declined like nouns (but note that тысяча has the instrumental тысячью). They are followed by a noun in the genitive plural.

ORDINAL NUMERALS

Ordinal numerals (e.g., пе́рвый, "first"; второ́й, "second"; тре́тий, "third") are declined like hard adjectives ending in -ый or -о́й and, like adjectives, must agree in gender, number and case with the modified noun. Thus: в пе́рвом до́ме ("in the first house"). Note, however, the special declension of тре́тий:

	SINGULAR			PLURAL
	MASC.	FEM.	NEUT.	ALL GENDERS
NOM.	тре́тий	тре́тья	тре́тье	тре́тьи
ACC.	тре́тий	тре́тью	тре́тье	тре́тьи
(ANIM.)	тре́тьего			тре́тьих
GEN.	тре́тьего	тре́тьей	тре́тьего	тре́тьих
DAT.	тре́тьему	тре́тьей	тре́тьему	тре́тьим
INSTR.	тре́тьим	тре́тьей	тре́тьим	тре́тьими
PREP.	тре́тьем	тре́тьей	тре́тьем	тре́тьих

APPENDIX III: DECLENSION OF NAMES

1. Russian first names (e.g., Ива́н, Со́ня) and patronymics (e.g., Ива́нович, Ива́новна) are declined like nouns.

2. Russian surnames ending in -ев, ёв, -ин, -ов or -ын are declined partly like nouns and partly like adjectives. Their full declension (using the model name Петро́в) is as follows:

	SINGULAR		PLURAL
	MASC.	FEM.	MASC. & FEM.
NOM.	Петро́в	Петро́ва	Петро́вы
ACC.	Петро́ва	Петро́ву	Петро́вых
GEN.	Петро́ва	Петро́вой	Петро́вых
DAT.	Петро́ву	Петро́вой	Петро́вым
INSTR.	Петро́вым	Петро́вой	Петро́выми
PREP.	Петро́ве	Петро́вой	Петро́вых

Surnames ending in -ский are declined like adjectives; those ending in -ко are usually not declined; those ending in -аго, -яго, -ово, -их, -ых and stressed -ко́ do not decline.

A GLOSSARY OF GRAMMATICAL TERMS

E. F. BLEILER

This section is intended to refresh your memory of grammatical terms or to clear up difficulties you may have had in understanding them. Before you work through the grammar, you should have a reasonably clear idea what the parts of speech and parts of a sentence are. This is not for reasons of pedantry, but simply because it is easier to talk about grammar if we agree upon terms. Grammatical terminology is as necessary to the study of grammar as the names of automobile parts are to garagemen.

This list is not exhaustive, and the definitions do not pretend to be complete, or to settle points of interpretation that grammarians have been disputing for the past several hundred years. It is a working analysis rather than a scholarly investigation. The definitions given, however, represent most typical American usage, and should serve for basic use.

The Parts of Speech

English words can be divided into eight important groups: nouns, adjectives, articles, verbs, adverbs, pronouns, prepositions and conjunctions. The boundaries between one group of words and another are sometimes vague and ill-felt in English, but a good dictionary, like the Webster Collegiate, can help you make decisions in questionable cases. Always bear in mind, however, that the way a word is used in a sentence may be just as important as the nature of the word itself in deciding what part of speech the word is.

Nouns. *Nouns* are the *words* for *things* of all *sorts*, whether these *things* are real *objects* that you can see, or *ideas*, or *places*, or *qualities* or *groups* or more abstract *things*. Examples of *words* that are *nouns* are *cat, vase, door, shrub, wheat, university, mercy, intelligence, ocean, plumber, pleasure, society, army.* If you are in *doubt* whether a given *word* is a *noun*, try putting the *word* "my," or "this" or "large" (or some other *adjective*) in *front* of it. If it makes *sense* in the *sentence* the *chances* are that the *word* in *question* is a *noun*. [All the *words* in *italics* in this *paragraph* are *nouns*.]

94

Adjectives. Adjectives are the words that delimit or give you *specific* information about the *various* nouns in a sentence. They tell you size, color, weight, pleasantness and many *other* qualities. *Such* words as *big, expensive, terrible, insipid, hot, delightful, ruddy, informative* are all *clear* adjectives. If you are in *any* doubt whether a *certain* word is an adjective, add "-er" to it, or put the word "more" or "too" in front of it. If it makes *good* sense in the sentence, and does not end in "-ly," the chances are that it is an adjective. (Pronoun-adjectives will be described under pronouns.) [The adjectives in the *above* sentences are in italics.]

Articles. There are only two kinds of articles in English, and they are easy to remember. The definite article is "the" and the indefinite article is "a" or "an."

Verbs. Verbs *are* the words that *tell* what action, or condition or relationship *is going* on. Such words as *was, is, jumps, achieved, keeps, buys, sells, has finished, run, will have, may, should pay, indicates are* all verb forms. *Observe* that a verb *can be composed* of more than one word, as *will have* and *should pay*, above; these *are called* compound verbs. As a rough guide for verbs, *try adding* "-ed" to the word you *are wondering* about, or *taking* off an "-ed" that *is* already there. If it *makes* sense, the chances *are* that it *is* a verb. (This *does* not always *work*, since the so-called strong or irregular verbs *make* forms by *changing* their middle vowels, like *spring, sprang, sprung*.) [Verbs in this paragraph *are* in italics.]

Adverbs. An adverb is a word that supplies additional information about a verb, an adjective or another adverb. It *usually* indicates time, or manner, or place or degree. It tells you *how*, or *when*, or *where* or to what degree things are happening. Such words as *now, then, there, not, anywhere, never, somehow, always, very* and most words ending in "-ly" are *ordinarily* adverbs. [Italicized words are adverbs.]

Pronouns. Pronouns are related to nouns, and take their place. (Some grammars and dictionaries group pronouns and nouns together as substantives.) *They* mention persons, or objects of any sort without actually giving their names.

   There are several different kinds of pronouns. (1) Personal pronouns: by a grammatical convention *I, we, me, mine, us, ours* are called first person pronouns, since *they* refer to the speaker; *you* and *yours* are called second person pronouns, since *they* refer to the person addressed; and *he, him, his, she, her, hers, they, them, theirs* are called third person pronouns, since *they* refer to the things or persons discussed. (2) Demonstrative pronouns: *this, that, these, those*. (3) Interrogative, or question, pronouns: *who, whom, what, whose, which*. (4) Relative pronouns, or pronouns *that* refer back to something already mentioned: *who, whom, that, which.* (5) Others: *some, any, anyone, no one, other, whichever, none,* etc.

Pronouns are difficult for *us,* since our categories are not as clear as in some other languages, and *we* use the same words for *what* foreign-language speakers see as different situations. First, our interrogative and relative pronouns overlap, and must be separated in translation. The easiest way is to observe whether a question is involved in the sentence. Examples: "*Which* [int.] do *you* like?" "The hotel, *which* [rel.] was not far from the airport, had a restaurant." "*Who* [int.] is there?" "*I* don't know *who* [int.] was there." "The porter *who* [rel.] took our bags was Number 2132." *This* may seem to be a trivial difference to an English speaker, but in some languages *it* is very important.

Secondly, there is an overlap between pronouns and adjectives. In some cases the word "this," for example, is a pronoun; in other cases *it* is an adjective. *This* also holds true for *his, its, her, any, none, other, some, that, these, those* and many other words. Note whether the word in question stands alone or is associated with another word. Examples: "*This* [pronoun] is mine." "This [adj.] taxi has no springs." Watch out for the word "that," which can be a pronoun or an adjective or a conjunction. And remember that "my," "your," "our" and "their" are always adjectives. [All pronouns in this section are in italics.]

Prepositions. Prepositions are the little words that introduce phrases that tell *about* condition, time, place, manner, association, degree and similar topics. Such words as *with, in, beside, under, of, to, about, for* and *upon* are prepositions. In English prepositions and adverbs overlap, but, as you will see *by* checking *in* your dictionary, there are usually differences *of* meaning *between* the two uses. [Prepositions *in* this paragraph are designated *by* italics.]

Conjunctions. Conjunctions are joining-words. They enable you to link words *or* groups of words into larger units, *and* to build compound *or* complex sentences out of simple sentence units. Such words as *and, but, although, or, unless* are typical conjunctions. *Although* most conjunctions are easy enough to identify, the word "that" should be watched closely to see *that* it is not a pronoun *or* an adjective. [Conjunctions italicized.]

Words About Verbs

Verbs are responsible for most of the terminology in this short grammar. The basic terms are:

Conjugation. In many languages verbs fall into natural groups, according to the way they make their forms. These groupings are called conjugations, and are an aid to learning grammatical structure. Though it may seem difficult at first to speak of First and Second Conjugations, these are simply short ways of saying that verbs belonging to these classes make their forms according to certain consistent rules, which you can memorize.

Infinitive. This is the basic form that most dictionaries give for verbs in most languages, and in most languages it serves as the basis for classifying verbs. In English (with a very few exceptions) it has no special form. To find the infinitive for any English verb, just fill in this sentence: "I like to........(walk, run, jump, swim, carry, disappear, etc.)." The infinitive in English is usually preceded by the word "to."

Tense. This is simply a formal way of saying "time." In English we think of time as being broken into three great segments: past, present and future. Our verbs are assigned forms to indicate this division, and are further subdivided for shades of meaning. We subdivide the present time into the present (I walk) and present progressive (I am walking); the past into the simple past (I walked), progressive past (I was walking), perfect or present perfect (I have walked), past perfect or pluperfect (I had walked); and future into simple future (I shall walk) and future progressive (I shall be walking). These are the most common English tenses.

Present Participles, Progressive (Continuous) Tenses. In English the present participle always ends in -*ing*. It can be used as a noun or an adjective in some situations, but its chief use is in *forming* the so-called progressive or continuous tenses. These are made by *putting* appropriate forms of the verb "to be" before a present participle. "To walk" [an infinitive], for example, has the present progressive: I am *walking*, you are *walking*, he is *walking*, etc.; past progressive, I was *walking*, you were *walking*, and so on. [Present participles are in italics.]

Past Participles, Perfect Tenses. The past participle in English is not *formed* as regularly as is the present participle. Sometimes it is *constructed* by adding "-ed" or "-d" to the present tense, as *walked, jumped, looked, received*; but there are many verbs where it is *formed* less regularly: *seen, been, swum, chosen, brought*. To find it, simply fill out the sentence "I have........," putting in the verb form that your ear tells you is right for the particular verb. If you speak grammatically, you will have the past participle.

Past participles are sometimes used as adjectives: "Don't cry over *spilt* milk." Their most important use, however, is to form the system of verb tenses that are *called* the perfect tenses: present perfect (or perfect), past perfect (or pluperfect), etc. In English the present perfect tense is *formed* with the present tense of "to have" and the past participle of a verb: I have *walked*, you have *run*, he has *begun*, etc. The past perfect is *formed*, similarly, with the past tense of "to have" and the past participle: I had *walked*, you had *run*, he had *begun*. Most of the languages you are likely to study have similar systems of perfect tenses, though they may not be *formed* in exactly the same way as in English. [Past participles are in italics.]

Auxiliary Verbs. Auxiliary verbs are special words that are used to help other verbs make their forms. In English, for example, we use forms of the verb "to have" to make our perfect tenses: I *have* seen, you *had* come, he *has* been, etc. We also use *shall* or *will* to make our future tenses: I *shall* pay, you *will* see, etc. French, German, Greek and Italian also make use of auxiliary verbs, but although the general concept is present, the use of auxiliaries differs very much from one language to another, and you *must* learn the practice for each language. [Auxiliary verbs are in italics.]

Reflexive. This term, which sounds more difficult than it really is, simply means that the verb flexes back upon the noun or pronoun that is its subject. In modern English the reflexive pronoun always has "-self" on its end, and we do not use the construction very frequently. In other languages, however, reflexive forms may be used more frequently, and in ways that do not seem very logical to an English speaker. Examples of English reflexive sentences: "He washes himself." "He seated himself at the table."

Passive. In some languages, like Latin, there is a strong feeling that an action or thing that is taking place can be expressed in two different ways. One can say, A does-something-to B, which is "active"; or B is-having-something-done-to-him by A, which is "passive." We do not have a strong feeling for this classification of experience in English, but the following examples should indicate the difference between an active and a passive verb: Active: "John is building a house." Passive: "A house is being built by John." Active: "The steamer carried the cotton to England." Passive: "The cotton was carried by the steamer to England." Bear in mind that the formation of passive verbs and the situations where they can be used vary enormously from language to language. This is one situation where you usually cannot translate English word for word into another language and make sense.

Impersonal Verbs. In English there are some verbs that do not have an ordinary subject, and do not refer to persons. They are always used with the pronoun "it," which does not refer to anything specifically, but simply serves to fill out the verb forms. Examples: "It is snowing." "It hailed last night." "It seems to me that you are wrong." "It has been raining." "It won't do."

Words About Nouns

Declensions. In some languages nouns fall into natural groups according to the way they make their forms. These groupings are called declensions, and making the various forms for any noun, pronoun or adjective is called declining it.

Declensions are simply an aid to learning grammatical structure. Although it may seem difficult to speak of First Declension, Second, Third and Fourth, these are simply short ways of saying that nouns belonging to these classes make their forms according to certain consistent rules, which you can memorize. In English we do not have to worry about declensions, since almost all nouns make their possessive and plural in the same way. In other languages, however, declensions may be much more complex.

Agreement. In some languages, where nouns or adjectives or articles are declined, or have gender endings, it is necessary that the adjective or article be in the same case or gender or number as the noun it goes with (modifies). This is called agreement.

This may be illustrated from Spanish, where articles and adjectives have to agree with nouns in gender and number:

una casa blanca	one white house	dos casas blancas	two white houses
un libro blanco	one white book	dos libros blancos	two white books

Here *una* is feminine singular and has the ending *-a* because it agrees with the feminine singular noun *casa*; *blanca* has the ending *-a* because it agrees with the feminine singular noun *casa*. *Blanco*, on the other hand, and *un* are masculine singular because *libro* is masculine singular.

Gender. Gender should not be confused with actual sex. In many languages nouns are arbitrarily assigned a gender (masculine or feminine, or masculine or feminine or neuter), and this need not correspond to sex. You simply have to learn the pattern of the language you are studying in order to become familiar with its use of gender.

Case. The idea of case is often very difficult for an English speaker to grasp, since we do not use case very much. Perhaps the best way to understand how case works is to step behind words themselves, into the ideas that words express. If you look at a sentence like "Mr. Brown is paying the waiter," you can see that three basic ideas are involved: Mr. Brown, the waiter and the act of payment. The problem that every language has is to show how these ideas are to be related, or how words are to be interlocked to form sentences.

Surprisingly enough, there are only three ways of putting pointers on words to make your meaning clear, so that your listener knows who is doing what to whom. These ways are: (1) word order; (2) additional words; (3) alteration of the word (which for nouns, pronouns and adjectives is called case).

Word order, or the place of individual words in a sentence, is very important in English. For us, "Mr. Brown is paying the waiter" is entirely different in meaning from "The waiter is paying Mr. Brown." This may seem so obvious that it need not be mentioned, but in some languages, like Latin, you can shift the positions of the words and come out with the same meaning for the sentence, apart from shifts of emphasis.

Adding other elements, to make meanings clear, is also commonly used in English. We have a whole range of words like "to," "from," "with," "in," "out," "of," and so on, that show relationships. "Mr. Jones introduced Mr. Smith to the Captain" is unambiguous because of the word "to."

Case is not as important in English as it is in some languages, but we do use case in a few limited forms. We add an -'s to nouns to form a possessive; we add a similar -s to form the plural for most nouns; and we add (in spelling, though there is no sound change involved) an -' to indicate a possessive plural. In pronouns, sometimes we add endings, as in the words "who," "whose" and "whom." Sometimes we use different forms, as in "I," "mine," "me"; "he," "his," "him"; "we," "ours" and "us."

When you use case, as you can see, you know much more about individual words than if you do not have case. When you see the word "whom" you automatically recognize that it cannot be the subject of a sentence, but must be the object of a verb or a preposition. When you see the word "ship's," you know that it means "belonging to a ship" or "originating from a ship."

If you assume that endings can be added to nouns or pronouns or adjectives to form cases, it is not too far a logical leap to see that certain forms or endings are always used in the same circumstances. A preposition, for example, may always be followed by a noun or pronoun with the same ending; a direct object may always have a certain ending; or possession may always be indicated by the same ending. If you classify and tabulate endings and their uses, you will arrive at individual cases.

Miscellaneous Terms

Comparative, Superlative. These two terms are used with adjectives and adverbs. They indicate the degree of strength within the meaning of the word. "Faster," "better," "earlier," "newer," "more rapid," "more detailed," "more suitable" are examples of the comparative in adjectives, while "more rapidly," "more recently," "more suitably" are comparatives for adverbs. In most cases, as you have seen, the comparative uses "-er" or "more" for an adjective, and "more" for an adverb. Superlatives are those forms that end in "-est" or have "most" prefixed before them for adjectives, and "most" prefixed for adverbs: "most intelligent," "earliest," "most rapidly," "most suitably."

The Parts of the Sentence

Subject, Predicate. In grammar *every complete sentence* contains two basic parts, the subject and the predicate. *The subject,* if *we* state the terms most simply, is the thing, person or activity talked about. *It* can be a noun, a pronoun, or something *that* serves as a noun. *A subject* would include, in a typical case, a noun, the articles or adjectives *that* are associated with it and perhaps phrases. Note that in complex sentences, *each part* may have its own subject. [*The subjects of the sentences and clauses above* have been italicized.]

The predicate *talks about the subject.* In a formal sentence the predicate *includes a verb, its adverbs, predicate adjectives, phrases and objects*— whatever *happens to be present.* A predicate adjective *is an adjective* that *happens to be in the predicate after a form of the verb "to be."* Example: "Apples *are red.*" [Predicates *are in italics.*]

In the following simple sentences subjects are in italics, predicates in italics and underlined. "*Green apples are bad for your digestion.*" "When *I go to Russia, I always stop in Novgorod.*" "*The man with the handbag is traveling to Moscow.*"

Direct and Indirect Objects. Some verbs (called transitive verbs) take direct and/or indirect objects in their predicates; other verbs (called intransitive verbs) do not take objects of any sort. In English, except for pronouns, objects do not have any special forms, but in languages such as Russian, which have case forms or more pronoun forms than English, objects can be troublesome.

The direct object is the person, thing, quality or matter that the verb directs *its action* upon. It can be a pronoun, or a noun, perhaps accompanied by an article and/or adjectives. The direct object always directly follows *its verb,* except when there is also an indirect object present, which comes between the verb and the object. Prepositions do not go before direct objects. Examples: "The cook threw *green onions* into the stew." "The border guards will want to see *your passport* tomorrow."

"Give *it* to me." "Please give me *a glass of red wine.*" [We have placed *direct objects* in this paragraph in italics.]

The indirect object, as grammars will tell *you,* is the person or thing for or to whom the action is taking place. It can be a pronoun or a noun with or without article and adjectives. In most cases the words "to" or "for" can be inserted before it, if not already there. Examples: "Please tell *me* the time." "I wrote *her* a letter from Pskov." "We sent *Mr. Chernyshev* ten rubles." "We gave *the most energetic guide* a large tip." [Indirect objects in this paragraph are in italics.]

Clauses: Independent, Dependent, Relative. Clauses are the largest components/*that go to make up sentences.*/ Each clause, in classical grammar, is a combination of subject and predicate./*If a sentence has one subject and one predicate,*/it is a one-clause sentence./*If it has two or more subjects and predicates,*/it is a sentence of two or more clauses./

There are two kinds of clauses: independent (principal) and dependent (subordinate) clauses./ An independent clause can stand alone;/it can form a logical, complete sentence./ A dependent clause is a clause/*that cannot stand alone;*/it must have another clause with it to complete it./

A sentence containing a single clause is called a simple sentence./ A sentence with two or more clauses may be either a complex or a compound sentence./ A compound sentence contains two or more independent clauses,/and/these independent clauses are joined together with "and," "or" or "but."/ A complex sentence is a sentence/*that contains both independent and dependent clauses.*/

A relative clause is a clause/*that begins with a relative pronoun: who, whom, that, which.*/ It is by definition a dependent clause,/*since it cannot stand by itself.*/

[Each clause in this section has been isolated by slashes./Dependent clauses have been placed in italics;/independent clauses have not been marked./]

INDEX

A CATALOG OF SELECTED
DOVER BOOKS
IN ALL FIELDS OF INTEREST

A CATALOG OF SELECTED DOVER
BOOKS IN ALL FIELDS OF INTEREST

CONCERNING THE SPIRITUAL IN ART, Wassily Kandinsky. Pioneering work by father of abstract art. Thoughts on color theory, nature of art. Analysis of earlier masters. 12 illustrations. 80pp. of text. 5⅜ x 8½. 23411-8

ANIMALS: 1,419 Copyright-Free Illustrations of Mammals, Birds, Fish, Insects, etc., Jim Harter (ed.). Clear wood engravings present, in extremely lifelike poses, over 1,000 species of animals. One of the most extensive pictorial sourcebooks of its kind. Captions. Index. 284pp. 9 x 12. 23766-4

CELTIC ART: The Methods of Construction, George Bain. Simple geometric techniques for making Celtic interlacements, spirals, Kells-type initials, animals, humans, etc. Over 500 illustrations. 160pp. 9 x 12. (Available in U.S. only.) 22923-8

AN ATLAS OF ANATOMY FOR ARTISTS, Fritz Schider. Most thorough reference work on art anatomy in the world. Hundreds of illustrations, including selections from works by Vesalius, Leonardo, Goya, Ingres, Michelangelo, others. 593 illustrations. 192pp. 7⅛ x 10¼. 20241-0

CELTIC HAND STROKE-BY-STROKE (Irish Half-Uncial from "The Book of Kells"): An Arthur Baker Calligraphy Manual, Arthur Baker. Complete guide to creating each letter of the alphabet in distinctive Celtic manner. Covers hand position, strokes, pens, inks, paper, more. Illustrated. 48pp. 8¼ x 11. 24336-2

EASY ORIGAMI, John Montroll. Charming collection of 32 projects (hat, cup, pelican, piano, swan, many more) specially designed for the novice origami hobbyist. Clearly illustrated easy-to-follow instructions insure that even beginning papercrafters will achieve successful results. 48pp. 8¼ x 11. 27298-2

THE COMPLETE BOOK OF BIRDHOUSE CONSTRUCTION FOR WOODWORKERS, Scott D. Campbell. Detailed instructions, illustrations, tables. Also data on bird habitat and instinct patterns. Bibliography. 3 tables. 63 illustrations in 15 figures. 48pp. 5¼ x 8½. 24407-5

BLOOMINGDALE'S ILLUSTRATED 1886 CATALOG: Fashions, Dry Goods and Housewares, Bloomingdale Brothers. Famed merchants' extremely rare catalog depicting about 1,700 products: clothing, housewares, firearms, dry goods, jewelry, more. Invaluable for dating, identifying vintage items. Also, copyright-free graphics for artists, designers. Co-published with Henry Ford Museum & Greenfield Village. 160pp. 8¼ x 11. 25780-0

HISTORIC COSTUME IN PICTURES, Braun & Schneider. Over 1,450 costumed figures in clearly detailed engravings–from dawn of civilization to end of 19th century. Captions. Many folk costumes. 256pp. 8⅜ x 11¾. 23150-X

STICKLEY CRAFTSMAN FURNITURE CATALOGS, Gustav Stickley and L. & J. G. Stickley. Beautiful, functional furniture in two authentic catalogs from 1910. 594 illustrations, including 277 photos, show settles, rockers, armchairs, reclining chairs, bookcases, desks, tables. 183pp. 6½ x 9¼. 23838-5

AMERICAN LOCOMOTIVES IN HISTORIC PHOTOGRAPHS: 1858 to 1949, Ron Ziel (ed.). A rare collection of 126 meticulously detailed official photographs, called "builder portraits," of American locomotives that majestically chronicle the rise of steam locomotive power in America. Introduction. Detailed captions. xi+ 129pp. 9 x 12. 27393-8

AMERICA'S LIGHTHOUSES: An Illustrated History, Francis Ross Holland, Jr. Delightfully written, profusely illustrated fact-filled survey of over 200 American lighthouses since 1716. History, anecdotes, technological advances, more. 240pp. 8 x 10¾. 25576-X

TOWARDS A NEW ARCHITECTURE, Le Corbusier. Pioneering manifesto by founder of "International School." Technical and aesthetic theories, views of industry, economics, relation of form to function, "mass-production split" and much more. Profusely illustrated. 320pp. 6⅛ x 9¼. (Available in U.S. only.) 25023-7

HOW THE OTHER HALF LIVES, Jacob Riis. Famous journalistic record, exposing poverty and degradation of New York slums around 1900, by major social reformer. 100 striking and influential photographs. 233pp. 10 x 7⅞. 22012-5

FRUIT KEY AND TWIG KEY TO TREES AND SHRUBS, William M. Harlow. One of the handiest and most widely used identification aids. Fruit key covers 120 deciduous and evergreen species; twig key 160 deciduous species. Easily used. Over 300 photographs. 126pp. 5⅜ x 8½. 20511-8

COMMON BIRD SONGS, Dr. Donald J. Borror. Songs of 60 most common U.S. birds: robins, sparrows, cardinals, bluejays, finches, more–arranged in order of increasing complexity. Up to 9 variations of songs of each species.
Cassette and manual 99911-4

ORCHIDS AS HOUSE PLANTS, Rebecca Tyson Northen. Grow cattleyas and many other kinds of orchids–in a window, in a case, or under artificial light. 63 illustrations. 148pp. 5⅜ x 8½. 23261-1

MONSTER MAZES, Dave Phillips. Masterful mazes at four levels of difficulty. Avoid deadly perils and evil creatures to find magical treasures. Solutions for all 32 exciting illustrated puzzles. 48pp. 8¼ x 11. 26005-4

MOZART'S DON GIOVANNI (DOVER OPERA LIBRETTO SERIES), Wolfgang Amadeus Mozart. Introduced and translated by Ellen H. Bleiler. Standard Italian libretto, with complete English translation. Convenient and thoroughly portable–an ideal companion for reading along with a recording or the performance itself. Introduction. List of characters. Plot summary. 121pp. 5¼ x 8½. 24944-1

TECHNICAL MANUAL AND DICTIONARY OF CLASSICAL BALLET, Gail Grant. Defines, explains, comments on steps, movements, poses and concepts. 15-page pictorial section. Basic book for student, viewer. 127pp. 5⅜ x 8½. 21843-0

THE CLARINET AND CLARINET PLAYING, David Pino. Lively, comprehensive work features suggestions about technique, musicianship, and musical interpretation, as well as guidelines for teaching, making your own reeds, and preparing for public performance. Includes an intriguing look at clarinet history. "A godsend," *The Clarinet,* Journal of the International Clarinet Society. Appendixes. 7 illus. 320pp. 5⅜ x 8½. 40270-3

HOLLYWOOD GLAMOR PORTRAITS, John Kobal (ed.). 145 photos from 1926-49. Harlow, Gable, Bogart, Bacall; 94 stars in all. Full background on photographers, technical aspects. 160pp. 8⅜ x 11¼. 23352-9

THE ANNOTATED CASEY AT THE BAT: A Collection of Ballads about the Mighty Casey/Third, Revised Edition, Martin Gardner (ed.). Amusing sequels and parodies of one of America's best-loved poems: Casey's Revenge, Why Casey Whiffed, Casey's Sister at the Bat, others. 256pp. 5⅜ x 8½. 28598-7

THE RAVEN AND OTHER FAVORITE POEMS, Edgar Allan Poe. Over 40 of the author's most memorable poems: "The Bells," "Ulalume," "Israfel," "To Helen," "The Conqueror Worm," "Eldorado," "Annabel Lee," many more. Alphabetic lists of titles and first lines. 64pp. 5³⁄₁₆ x 8¼. 26685-0

PERSONAL MEMOIRS OF U. S. GRANT, Ulysses Simpson Grant. Intelligent, deeply moving firsthand account of Civil War campaigns, considered by many the finest military memoirs ever written. Includes letters, historic photographs, maps and more. 528pp. 6⅛ x 9¼. 28587-1

ANCIENT EGYPTIAN MATERIALS AND INDUSTRIES, A. Lucas and J. Harris. Fascinating, comprehensive, thoroughly documented text describes this ancient civilization's vast resources and the processes that incorporated them in daily life, including the use of animal products, building materials, cosmetics, perfumes and incense, fibers, glazed ware, glass and its manufacture, materials used in the mummification process, and much more. 544pp. 6⅛ x 9¼. (Available in U.S. only.) 40446-3

RUSSIAN STORIES/RUSSKIE RASSKAZY: A Dual-Language Book, edited by Gleb Struve. Twelve tales by such masters as Chekhov, Tolstoy, Dostoevsky, Pushkin, others. Excellent word-for-word English translations on facing pages, plus teaching and study aids, Russian/English vocabulary, biographical/critical introductions, more. 416pp. 5⅜ x 8½. 26244-8

PHILADELPHIA THEN AND NOW: 60 Sites Photographed in the Past and Present, Kenneth Finkel and Susan Oyama. Rare photographs of City Hall, Logan Square, Independence Hall, Betsy Ross House, other landmarks juxtaposed with contemporary views. Captures changing face of historic city. Introduction. Captions. 128pp. 8¼ x 11. 25790-8

AIA ARCHITECTURAL GUIDE TO NASSAU AND SUFFOLK COUNTIES, LONG ISLAND, The American Institute of Architects, Long Island Chapter, and the Society for the Preservation of Long Island Antiquities. Comprehensive, well-researched and generously illustrated volume brings to life over three centuries of Long Island's great architectural heritage. More than 240 photographs with authoritative, extensively detailed captions. 176pp. 8¼ x 11. 26946-9

NORTH AMERICAN INDIAN LIFE: Customs and Traditions of 23 Tribes, Elsie Clews Parsons (ed.). 27 fictionalized essays by noted anthropologists examine religion, customs, government, additional facets of life among the Winnebago, Crow, Zuni, Eskimo, other tribes. 480pp. 6⅛ x 9¼. 27377-6

CATALOG OF DOVER BOOKS

THE STORY OF THE TITANIC AS TOLD BY ITS SURVIVORS, Jack Winocour (ed.). What it was really like. Panic, despair, shocking inefficiency, and a little heroism. More thrilling than any fictional account. 26 illustrations. 320pp. 5⅜ x 8½.
20610-6

FAIRY AND FOLK TALES OF THE IRISH PEASANTRY, William Butler Yeats (ed.). Treasury of 64 tales from the twilight world of Celtic myth and legend: "The Soul Cages," "The Kildare Pooka," "King O'Toole and his Goose," many more. Introduction and Notes by W. B. Yeats. 352pp. 5⅜ x 8½.
26941-8

BUDDHIST MAHAYANA TEXTS, E. B. Cowell and others (eds.). Superb, accurate translations of basic documents in Mahayana Buddhism, highly important in history of religions. The Buddha-karita of Asvaghosha, Larger Sukhavativyuha, more. 448pp. 5⅜ x 8½.
25552-2

ONE TWO THREE . . . INFINITY: Facts and Speculations of Science, George Gamow. Great physicist's fascinating, readable overview of contemporary science: number theory, relativity, fourth dimension, entropy, genes, atomic structure, much more. 128 illustrations. Index. 352pp. 5⅜ x 8½.
25664-2

EXPERIMENTATION AND MEASUREMENT, W. J. Youden. Introductory manual explains laws of measurement in simple terms and offers tips for achieving accuracy and minimizing errors. Mathematics of measurement, use of instruments, experimenting with machines. 1994 edition. Foreword. Preface. Introduction. Epilogue. Selected Readings. Glossary. Index. Tables and figures. 128pp. 5⅜ x 8½. 40451-X

DALÍ ON MODERN ART: The Cuckolds of Antiquated Modern Art, Salvador Dalí. Influential painter skewers modern art and its practitioners. Outrageous evaluations of Picasso, Cézanne, Turner, more. 15 renderings of paintings discussed. 44 calligraphic decorations by Dalí. 96pp. 5⅜ x 8½. (Available in U.S. only.)
29220-7

ANTIQUE PLAYING CARDS: A Pictorial History, Henry René D'Allemagne. Over 900 elaborate, decorative images from rare playing cards (14th–20th centuries): Bacchus, death, dancing dogs, hunting scenes, royal coats of arms, players cheating, much more. 96pp. 9¼ x 12¼.
29265-7

MAKING FURNITURE MASTERPIECES: 30 Projects with Measured Drawings, Franklin H. Gottshall. Step-by-step instructions, illustrations for constructing handsome, useful pieces, among them a Sheraton desk, Chippendale chair, Spanish desk, Queen Anne table and a William and Mary dressing mirror. 224pp. 8⅛ x 11¼.
29338-6

THE FOSSIL BOOK: A Record of Prehistoric Life, Patricia V. Rich et al. Profusely illustrated definitive guide covers everything from single-celled organisms and dinosaurs to birds and mammals and the interplay between climate and man. Over 1,500 illustrations. 760pp. 7½ x 10⅛.
29371-8

Paperbound unless otherwise indicated. Available at your book dealer, online at www.doverpublications.com, or by writing to Dept. GI, Dover Publications, Inc., 31 East 2nd Street, Mineola, NY 11501. For current price information or for free catalogues (please indicate field of interest), write to Dover Publications or log on to www.doverpublications.com and see every Dover book in print. Dover publishes more than 500 books each year on science, elementary and advanced mathematics, biology, music, art, literary history, social sciences, and other areas.